D1823849

# Byron and Scott

Drawing Room at Fifty Albemarle Street. Watercolour by L. Werner c.1850.
Courtesy of The John Murray Collection

# Byron and Scott:
## The Waverley Novels
## and Historical Engagement

By

## Roderick S. Speer

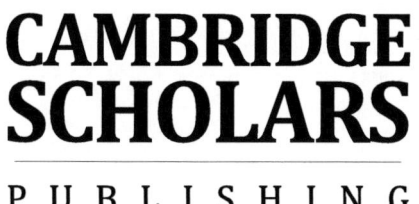

**CAMBRIDGE**
**SCHOLARS**
P U B L I S H I N G

Byron and Scott: The Waverley Novels and Historical Engagement, by Roderick S. Speer

This book first published 2009

Cambridge Scholars Publishing

12 Back Chapman Street, Newcastle upon Tyne, NE6 2XX, UK

British Library Cataloguing in Publication Data
A catalogue record for this book is available from the British Library

ISBN (10): 1-4438-0587-4, ISBN (13): 978-1-4438-0587-2

# TABLE OF CONTENTS

# PREFACE AND ACKNOWLEDGMENTS

First, on text citations. My publisher has wisely adhered to the principal of, 'Whatever you do, be consistent,' with minimal expression of definite preferences, though these did exist. But in trying to be consistent, I have found little support, even from 'definitive' sources. For example, Canto stanza numbers are expressed in Arabic numerals, sometimes with a period, sometimes without in the definitive source. I have used the latter form only. For drama citations I have simply used a pointed numeral style, e.g. I.ii.335-36.

In terms of acknowlegments, my first goes to the scholar who tweaked my interest in Lord Byron, retired Professor Gabriele B. Jackson of Temple University in Philadelphia, Pennsylvania, U.S.A., who departed from her Ben Jonson area to conduct a Byron seminar at the University of Pennsylvania, and found at least one responding scholar. I must also record a tribute to that great Scottish man of letters, Angus Calder, whose mention of my 'Byron and the Scottish Literary Tradition' in a 1989 University of Edinburgh Press book, led to my revival of activity in the Byron arena. Angus has since passed, but not before we met in Edinburgh on two occasions in the 2006 time period. Thanks for this connection go to that noted literary bean-counter and devoted Byronist, Eric Wishart of Edinburgh. They also certainly go to the first distinguished scholar who knew of my line on Byron and Scott, Byronist John Clubbe, and to leading Byron scholar, Peter Cochran. To Harriet Cullen and the KEATS-SHELLEY REVIEW, who saw fit to award me their second prize in the 2007 Essay Contest for what appears here as Part Two of Chapter One, albeit with a slightly revised conclusion. And to that essential infrastructure offered by the International Byron Society, its English face, Alan Rawes at Manchester, and its American, Charles Robinson, University of Delaware, for prompt support and responses. All would be so halting and difficult, without these true helpmates of Byron scholarship, though none had any hand in the writing of the book itself.

I record appreciation to Paul Davies of Carlisle, Pennsylvania and James K. Dempsey, of Covington, Kentucky for computer support. I must also thank the euphoniously named—for a retired English professor—Keats Sparrow of East Carolina University, for his forbearance in my pursuing matters Byronic in a respite from editing the papers of the great North Carolina Revolutionary, Richard Caswell.

I also salute the seventh generation John Murray for allowing use of the Fifty Albemarle Street picture from the John Murray collection. And as always, to my wife Virginia, for tolerating my absorption in this enterprise.

In earlier times, I had academic affiliations with the University of Pennsylvania and with Huron College of the University of Western Ontario, Canada. In more recent times, I have not had an academic affiliation, but rather institutional ones: to the Fenwick Library of George Mason University and the George Mason District Library, both in Fairfax County, Virginia; and to the Library of Congress, Washington, D.C., for their provision of superb collections or finding services. Lastly, the kind patience of the Cambridge Scholars Publishing crew, Carol Koulikourdi, my editor; Amanda Millar, my understanding typesetter who tolerated the fact I am no Word expert; and Soucin Yip-Sou, graphics editor *sans pereil*.

# INTRODUCTION

# BACKGROUND AND PROCEDURE

In the nineteenth century, Byron and Scott were often cast as opposites. Hazlitt criticized Byron for falling short of Scott's objectivity, for casting his descriptions 'in the mould of his own individual impressions' rather than 'in the mould of nature' as Scott had done.[1] Carlyle found such subjectivity in Byron exemplary of 'the diseased self-conscious state of Literature,' while Ruskin praised Scott for his faithfulness to the object, his 'unselfishness and humility.'[2] John Nichol reported that in the decades before 1860, Scott and Byron were 'perpetually contrasted as representatives of the manly and morbid schools.'[3] Leslie Stephen replaced such Manichaean oppositions with the more generous concept of complementarity, but still saw the two writers as opposites:

> If Byron and Scott could have been combined; if the energetic passions of the one could have been joined to the healthy nature and quick sympathies of the other, we might have seen another Shakespeare in the nineteenth century. As it is, both of them are maimed and imperfect on different sides.[4]

The first significant criticism of Scott in the twentieth century, that of the Marxist, Georg Lukacs, found essentially the same polarity as Hazlitt, attacking Byron for maintaining a 'lyrical-subjectivist absolute' and praising Scott for his objectivity and socio-historical concern.[5]

In these critical pairings of Byron and Scott, the two are polarized, and critic and reader are usually forced to choose sides without exploring the possibility that one author could have influenced the other. The fact that Scott's most important work is agreed to be in the novel and Byron's, of course, in poetry has further tended to discourage comparative studies of these authors; instead, students have retreated, each to his preferred genre. Biographers, however, have had to acknowledge that Byron and Scott enjoyed a close friendship from 1815, when they met, to the end of their lives. Leslie Marchand finds the friendship 'curious,' and one of Scott's recent biographers memorably calls it 'queer but sincere.'[6] John Nichol in

1880 seemed to sense in their friendship a significance inconsistent with the fact that Byron and Scott were 'for a season perpetually pitted against one another, as the foremost competitors for literary favour,' and belying the subsequent critical contrasting of them. He concludes, 'The fact therefore that from an early period the men themselves knew each other as they were, is worth illustrating. . . .'[7] Nichol illustrates by examining the correspondence between them and concludes that their praise of each other is not flattery, for they spoke of each other to third parties in the same way. While 'illustrating' the friendship of the two, Nichol does not develop its implications, biographical or critical. R. W. Chambers later suggested a biographical benefit in such an inquiry, by way of defending Byron's humane nature:

> His relations with Scott show how chivalrous he could be in dealing with men of politics and temper different from his own. ... more profit is to be got out of thinking of Byron's friendship with Scott than by giving historic value to his libels upon Castlereagh or Southey.[8]

The call for a study of the humane Byron has been virtually answered by G. Wilson Knight who defends 'Byron's true greatness, his generosity and kindliness, his chivalry, courtesy, humility and courage.'[9] Although these are qualities traditionally ascribed to Scott, Knight does not treat the friendship with Scott at all. Byron scholars received Knight's study snappishly, claiming it did not show the whole Byron. It did, however, show a side of Byron that had always been neglected, and one to which Scott testified.

If Knight's revision of traditional views of Byron (as gloomy, perverse, diabolic) brought Byron closer to the personality usually ascribed to Scott, closer attention to Scott's private life and especially his post-bankruptcy *Journal* have made him seem more like the old Byron. Christina Keith's provocative biographical study finds Scott a man of enigma, duplicity, amorality, and Bohemianism. She asserts that Byron 'probably fitted in to every facet of Scott's many-sided personality more closely than anyone else Scott ever met.'[10]

Such revisions of the traditional biographical contrarieties concerning Byron and Scott raise the possibility that the critical contrarieties also may have been misconceptions. Recent critical comparisons of Byron and of Scott treat mainly of the personal relationship, but stop short and only suggest some possible literary implications of the relationship.[11] The study presented here, in addition to showing that the friendship of Byron and Scott was no anomaly, argues that the impact of Scott's literary endeavors and direction on Byron was more considerable than has been assumed. The study falls into two major sections: Chapter ONE, which examines the apparent effect of Scott, his novels, and the ethos of Scotland which they invoked, on Byron's life; and four subsequent chapters, which examine the possible effects on his poetry. An influence of Scott on Byron is implied, but since of course no provable direct causal relation is provable, we have the benefits of at least a comparative study, wherein 'A fund of insights becomes available which might escape direct approach.'[12]

Chapter ONE establishes a biographical base for considering the effect of Scott and his works on Byron. The meeting of the two writers in 1815 and their affinities are discussed. One of these, their Scottish background, seems to have been of especial importance to Byron: that he continued throughout his life to be imaginatively sustained by things Scottish helps explain his extraordinary enthusiasm for Scott and his novels. Scott put Byron in touch with the positive ideals of his boyhood, ideals essential for Byron's turn to a life of action and to the depiction of heroes active in the crises of history. Scott's novels, with their presentation of heroes braving historical crisis, served as models for this new orientation of Byron's life and art.

Chapter TWO reviews Byron's poetry before 1814 to show that it was not the characteristic utterance of a man of historical action: the 'Byronic Heroes' of this work operate on a suprahistorical plane. Scott's early writing, his verse romances, is reviewed to show how he moved away from melodrama to historical fiction, a development culminating in his Waverley novels. After becoming an avid reader of Scott's novels, Byron also turned to the examination of historical situations and heroes involved in the sociopolitical crises of their times. The last three chapters examine in detail Byron's major explorations of historical involvement, in three bodies of work: the Historical Dramas, *Don Juan*, and *The Island*.

Chapter THREE shows that in the Historical Dramas—*Marino Faliero, Sardanapalus,*. and *The Two Foscari*—Byron depicts three varieties of Byronic Hero: the irascible Marino Faliero, the epicurean Sardanapalus, and the stoical Doge Francis Foscari. It is only in the third case that Byron develops a hero with the qualities necessary for significant involvement in the affairs of the world. Byron's uneven handling of the hero in historical crisis is a token of the unsuitability of the Byronic Hero for such involvement. Scott's relatively successful handling of Henry Morton in *Old Mortality* is presented for contrast.

Chapter FOUR argues for a comparison of *Don* Juan's Juan with the typical modest hero of Scott's novels, as exemplified by Edward Waverley of *Waverley*. It is concluded that Juan has been underrated as a hero, and that he exhibits qualities central to Byron's developing concept of heroism.

Chapter FIVE argues that in *The Island* Byron produced his most Scottian work, for he depicted both the Byronic Hero's destruction and the modest hero's transcendence of the terrors of history. Scott's themes and approaches are compared.

An Afterword brings this biographical-critical study to a close, noting Byron's plunge into the Greek war of independence, and concluding that Scott and his novels played an important part in the development of Byron's life and works. In placing on common ground two writers so frequently assumed to be antithetical, I have hoped to add to the coherence of our view of the major Romantics, and perhaps to have brought a new perspective to the charge that Byron had 'an uncritical regard for the novels of Walter Scott.'[13]

# Notes

[1] *The Spirit of the Age* (1825; rpt. London: Oxford Univ. Press, 1954), p. 106.

[2] Thomas Carlyle, 'Characteristics' (1831), *The Works of Thomas Carlyle*. ed. H. D. Traill, Centenary Edition, 30 vols. (New York: Scribner's, 1899) 28 , 24; and John Ruskin, *Modern Painters* (1856) 3, Part 4, Ch. xvi, 'Of Modern Language,' *The Works of John Ruskin*. ed. E. T. Cook and Alexander Wedderburn, Library Edition, 39 vols. (London: Allen, 1903-12) 4, 342.

[3] Byron. E.M.O.L. Series (London: Macmillan, 1880), p.79.

[4] 'Some Words about Sir Walter Scott' (1871; rpt. Hours *in .a Library,* London: Smith, Elder, 1876), p. 278.

[5] Georg Lukacs, *The Historical Novel* . 2nd ed., trans. Hannah and Stanley Mitchell (London: Merlin Press, 1962), p. 34.

[6] Marchand, *Byron: A Biography* (New York: Knopf, 1957), II, 530; Hesketh Pearson, Walter Scott: *His Life and Personality* (London: Methuen, 1954), 106.

[7] *Byron,* 78-79.

[8] 'Ruskin (and others) on Byron,' English Association Pamphlet no. 62, Nov. 1925.

[9] *Lord Byron: Christian Virtues* (New York: Barnes & Noble, 1953), p. 29.

[10] *The Author of Waverley: A Study in the Personality of Sir Walter Scott* (London: Robert Hale, 1964).

[11] John Clubbe, in 'Byron and Scott,' *Texas Studies in Language and Literature*, 1973, stresses the friendship and declines to pursue 'any reciprocal literary influence,' although he does suggest some connections, such as the appreciation of the truths in history. Andrew Rutherford in 'Byron, Scott, and Scotland,' in *Lord Byron and his Contemporaries*, ed. Charles E. Robinson, (Newark: Univ. of Delaware Press 1982), pp. 34-65, likewise stresses the congeniality of the two men, but helpfully draws a comparison between Byron's life and that of Scott's

young Waverley heroes. The present study keeps the biographical context in mind while exploring the literary concepts of heroship of both writers.

[12] Mark Spilka, *Dickens and Kafka: a Mutual Interpretation* (London: D.Dobson, 1963), p. 23.

[13] Editorial comment in Leslie A. Marchand, ed., *Byron's Letters and Journals* (Cambridge: Harvard Univ. Press, 1973-1982), 16 vols. 3, 271. Hereafter, *BLJ.*

Byron in the Highlands © Currier & Ives

# CHAPTER ONE

# ORIGIN AND RETURN:
# BYRON, SCOTT, AND SCOTLAND

Breathes there the man with soul so dead,
Who never to himself hath said,
This is my own, my native land!
—Scott, *The Lay of the Last Minstrel*

## Part I: Byron's Meeting with Scott

We have a memorable vignette of Byron and Scott on the occasion of
their first meeting, at John Murray's office in April 1815:

> After Scott and he had ended their conversation in the drawing-room, it
> was a curious sight to see the two greatest poets of the age—both lame—
> stumping downstairs side by side. They continued to meet together in
> Albemarle Street nearly every day, and remained together for two or three
> hours at a time.[1]

Two points are brought out in this brief description which suggest part
of the basis for the two men's intimacy at the Albemarle Street meetings
and for their subsequent lifelong fascination for and allegiance to each
other.

First, Byron and Scott were 'the two greatest poets of the age,' at least
in terms of public acclaim. We know how Byron after publishing the first
two cantos of *Childe Harold* in 1812 had 'awakened to find myself
famous.'[2] His subsequent 'Oriental Tales' with their exotic, conscience-
afflicted heroes further fired the public fascination with Byron. Scott's
popularity was of longer standing, having begun with *The Lay of the Last
Minstrel* in 1805, and continued with *Marmion* (1808) and *The Lady of the
Lake* (1810). In 1813 Byron commented in his *Journal* that Scott 'is
undoubtedly the Monarch of Parnassus.'[3] In a later *Journal* comment,
Byron was curiously self-effacing on hearing his name coupled with
Scott's, for he felt it 'a compliment—though I think Scott deserves better
company.'[4] By the time Byron and Scott were in company at Murray's,

Scott's own verse had become less popular, largely because of Byron's superior Tales. Because of this decline in popularity—Scott's famous explanation was that 'Byron *bet* me'[5]—but more importantly because of the aesthetic demands of his own development, Scott had turned to prose fiction with *Waverlev* (1814) and entered a period of new and greater popularity. Although the authorship of *Wayerley* was anonymous, Byron for one believed it was by Walter Scott and was very enthusiastic about it.[6]

Since Scott was Byron's literary peer in respect of popularity, he was above the crowd of lionizers who were always besieging Byron. Lady Blessington explains:

> Circumstances had rendered Byron suspicious; he was apt to attribute every mark of interest or good-will shown to him as emanating from vanity, that sought gratification by a contact with his poetical celebrity. . . . But as Sir W. Scott's own well-earned celebrity put the possibility of such a motive out of the question, Byron yielded to the sentiment of friendship in all its force for him, and never named him but with praise and affection.[7]

A second point made by John Murray, Jr., is that both writers were lame. Byron's lameness has been viewed by many scholars as the cause of his sense of bitterness and personal isolation from the earliest age. Scott's lameness has not usually been remarked upon, however, because it does not seem to jibe with the conventional view of his supposedly benign personality and works.

One exception among his works, which John Gibson Lockhart singles out, is *The Black Dwarf* (1816), in which we encounter the feelings of a misanthropic, hunchbacked dwarf,

> the dark feelings so often connected with physical deformity; feelings which appear to have diffused their shadow over the whole genius of Byron—and which, but for this singular picture, we should hardly have conceived ever to have passed through Scott's happier mind.[8]

Lockhart, approaching Byron and Scott in a Manichaean way, refuses to see their points in common. The later biographer, Christina Keith, sees in Scott not a happy man, but a secretive one, his whole life marked by his early response to his brothers' taunting of his lameness:

> The sensitive child who hid all his real feelings from the scorn of his coarser brothers became the man who hid his partnership with the Ballantines from the scorn of the aristocratic legal world. The child who read Shakespeare in secret by firelight became the man who wrote the Waverley Novels in secret and denied their authorship.[9]

From Scott's lameness, too, came his frustration in young manhood at being unable to go to the French wars—the origin, perhaps, of his great amateur's interest in warfare. Feelings of inadequacy may well have motivated his creation of that monument of neo-feudal grandeur, Abbotsford. Furthermore, a dark vision of life is revealed by those works which Scott produced under physical or emotional stress—*The Bride of Lammermoor* (1819), written in the delirium of sickness, the *Journal* entries made under the pressure of the 1825 bankruptcy; this vision is unlike that of the better known (and more numerous) novels with happy endings. Scott's lameness, then, quite possibly played a more considerable part in his life than we have been accustomed to think.

In addition to the literary eminence and physical lameness commented on by Murray, Byron and Scott shared a dislike for pure *literati* and saw each other as men of wider experiences. Scott made the point in his 6 November letter to Byron, when he criticized Southey:

> . . . every atom of his soul and every moment of his time dedicated to literary pursuits, in which he differs from almost all those who have divided public attention with him. Your Lordship's habits of society, for example, and my own professional and official avocations, must necessarily connect us much more with our respective classes in the usual routine of pleasure or business, than if we had not any other employment than *vacare musis*.[10]

Byron at times had felt Scott to be too lacking in experience.[11] But he agreed with Scott's depreciation of literary men and came to exclude him from their number:

> In general, I do not draw well with literary men—not that I dislike them, but 1 never know what to say to them after 1 have praised their last publication—There are several exceptions, to be sure; but then they have either been men of the world such as Scott—and Moore &c or visionaries out of it—such as Shelley &c....[12]

Along with these deep agreements in perspective were to be found Byron and Scott's shared humaneness, social charm, and sense of humor.[13] These qualities put both men beyond the range of differences in politics and supposedly of personality which so many commentators seem to have expected should have divided them.[14] Once their friendship had begun, there was a matter which was to prove of growing importance to Byron: their shared Scottish background. Scott in his person and his works came to serve as a link for Byron between his life in exile (after 1816) and his childhood in Scotland. That Byron valued such a link revealed his need to return to the idealism of his boyhood as a basis for a new life and poetry. The ethos of Scotland early felt by Byron and then returned to through the medium of Scott and his novels may now be explored.

## Part II: Scotland in Byron's Life and Poetry

Legally speaking, of course, Byron was English, born in line to the English peerage, heir to Newstead Abbey in Nottinghamshire, and educated after the age of ten in England. Scotland is pertinent to Byron's life on the basis of his having spent early boyhood, from the age of two to the age of ten (1790-98), in Aberdeen with his mother.[15] When Scott wrote Byron in 1812 of 'Scotland which has a maternal claim on you,' he was not personifying Scotland but referring to Byron's mother, the former Catherine Gordon of Gight, whose family name Byron bore.[16] As Byron was to express it in *Don Juan*, he was 'half a Scot by birth, and bred a whole one' (X.17).[17] He first knew himself as 'little Geordie,' and as a boy is reported to have stressed his Scottish name, calling himself 'George Byron Gordon.'[18] He spoke with a thick Scots accent, for his widowed mother's poor financial situation did not permit social isolation from the uneducated classes who spoke Scots.

The whole environment of his Aberdeen years conditioned him to the views of the lower-middleclass Scottish world with which he was daily associated in the streets and later at school.[19] Byron later explained another important feature of his life in Scotland. When he was eight, 'after an attack of the scarlet fever at Aberdeen, I was removed by medical advice into the Highlands. Here I passed occasionally some summers, and from this period I date my love of mountainous countries.'[20] This love is first asserted in Byron's early lyrics.

Published in several volumes from 1806 to 1808 and collectively referred to now as 'Hours of Idleness,' Byron's early poems show him practicing many voices and playing many roles. The roles significant to this essay are two, from two groups of poems: the Scottish-set poems, 'Lachin y Gair,' 'I Would I Were a Careless Child,' and 'When I Roved a Young Highlander,' in which the speaker is a young boy; and the Newstead Abbey poems, 'Elegy on Newstead Abbey' and 'To an Oak at Newstead,' in which the speaker pictures himself as the last 'heir of a noble tradition.'

The three Scottish poems fit the general pattern in 'Hours of Idleness' of a nostalgic return to the happier conditions of childhood. But here the happier conditions are not those of a lost Eden of abundance or innocence, but rather of a lost tradition of heroic struggle, expressed in terms of the Scottish national wars with England. In 'Lachin y Gair,' the Scottish Highlands are contrasted with the England of the poet's present. Byron focuses on topographical symbolism: Scotland's mountainous, wild, uncultivated landscape, while lacking in fruitfulness, is nevertheless preferable—'I loved my bleak regions' he says in 'When I Roved' (st. 2)—to a garden like England, 'tame and domestic' (st. 5). The greatness of the Highlands results from the race of men bred there,the 'chieftains, long perish'd' (st.2). who have proven the value of the place by their struggles. Their spirits populate the setting:

> 'Shades of the dead! have I not heard your voices
> Rise on the night-rolling breath of the gale?'
>                         (st. 3)

The poet identifies with the dead warriors through Ancestry, calling them 'the forms of my fathers.' They represent for him a noble response to the human condition for they died at Culloden in defiance of fate. 'Ill-starr'd, though brave' (st. 4). In 'I Would I Were,' the English-Scottish contrast is articulated as being between those who are heavy in spirit and slavish and the Highlander with his 'freeborn soul' (st. 1). To die fated though free is thus seen as preferable to a servile security. The values of Highland life expressed in these Scottish poems are consistent with Byron's lifelong exploration of man's fated condition and are far from a weakly sentimental nostalgia.

Newstead Abbey, on the other hand, seems to symbolize man's capitulation to such fatedness. The Newstead Abbey poems are in a melancholy, elegiac style, and while the history of the poet's forebears and of the Abbey is recounted fully in 'Elegy on Newstead Abbey,' the weight of this poem and 'To an Oak at Newstead' comes down on a decadent present, not a glorious past:

> The last and youngest of a noble line,
> Now holds thy mouldering turrets in his sway.
>                         (st. 35)

The Elegy ends with the weak hope that 'Hours, splendid as the past, may still be thine' (st. 39), but the narrator does not seem personally involved in this resurrection; in 'Oak' he hopes merely to be revered in his grave by posterity. Nowhere is the melancholy graveyard tone broken by a passionate cry like that of 'Lachin,' 'Oh! for the crags that are wild and majestic' (st. 5).

The Scottish poems thus seem central to the poetry Byron was yet to write. An exultant sense of personal freedom in defiance of fatedness is exemplified by the heroes of all Byron's serious, non-satiric poems, and by the narrator of *Childe Harold*. The importance of Scotland as the first setting for this basic vision should not, therefore, be underemphasized. Byron in 1807 even contemplated making a collection of folk ballads to be called *The Highland Harp.*[21]

However, the young Byron was to suffer, as so often in his life, public censure for his self-exposure. The result was a period of public concealment of his affections for Scotland, lasting until the development of his friendship with Scott. This period is worth examining briefly, for it would appear on the face of it that Byron came completely to hate Scott and Scotland.

Byron had written reverently of his ancestry and of Scotland; the *Edinburgh* reviewer censured both his egocentricity and his misuse of a Scots word:

> There is a good deal also about his maternal ancestors, in a Poem on Lachin-y-gair, a mountain where he spent part of his youth, and might have learnt that *pibroch* is not a bagpipe, any more than duet means a fiddle.[22]

Byron thus stood accused of affectation in his feelings and knowledge about Scotland. (To be fair, the reviewer might have noted the use of a distinctly Scots pronunciation in the poem criticized, in lines ten and twelve, where 'plaid' has the long 'a' to rhyme with 'glade.') Byron felt himself 'cut to atoms' by the review.[23] Ethel Colburn Mayne asks whether we can doubt, 'on even slender knowledge of him, that during that turmoil Scotland became the very Hades?' and goes on to recount an incident as evidence:

> A girl, at the time of the notorious article, happened to observe that she thought he had a slight Scotch accent. 'Good God' he cried, on hearing of it, 'I hope not. I would rather the d—d country was sunk in the sea. I, the Scotch accent!'

Moore's account of the incident has Byron in only half playful rage, and explains Byron's syndrome in such moments of crisis:

> Cordial, however, and deep as were the impressions which he retained of Scotland, he would sometimes in this, as in all his other amiable feelings, endeavour perversely to belie his own better nature; and, when under the excitement of anger or ridicule, persuade not only others, but even himself, that the whole current of his feelings ran directly otherwise. The abuse

with which, in his anger against the Edinburgh Review, he overwhelmed everything Scotch, is an instance of this temporary triumph of wilfulness.[24]

Byron's willfulness in defending himself against a hostile world achieved literary form in *English Bards and Scotch Reviewers* (1809), where he attacked the contemporary literary establishment for its debased values. He took a position on Scott and his poetry, and on the concepts of nationalism and literature. Both positions are relevant to the question of Byron's affirmation of his Scottishness: on the one hand we find Byron dissociating himself from literary provincialism, that is, a specifically Scottish literature; on the other, we find him making the first, albeit negative, move toward a relationship with Scott, a relationship which would ultimately return Byron to that sense of his Scottishness which he now seemed so eager to disavow.

While Byron treated Scott more favorably than he did his other contemporaries, his praise was ambiguous. He did not like Scott's *The Lay of the Last Minstrel*: 'Lays of Minstrels—may they be the last!—I On half-strung harps whine mournful to the blast' (11.153-54). His ambivalent description of *Marmion* reflected contemporary criticism of it for being irreverent in its depiction of medieval knighthood:

> Next view in state, proud prancing on his roan,
> The golden-crested haughty Marmion,
> Now forging scrolls, now foremost in the fight,
> Not quite a Felon, yet but half a Knight,
> The gibbet or the field prepared to grace;
> A mighty mixture of the great and base.
> (11. 165-70)

Responding to accounts of Scott's commercial success with these verse romances, Byron then attacked Scott *ad hominem*:

> And think'st thou, SCOTT! by vain conceit perchance,
> On public taste to foist thy stale romance,
> Though MURRAY with his MILLER may combine
> To yield thy muse just half-a-crown per line?
> No! when the sons of song descend to trade,
> Their bays are sear, their former laurels fade,
> Let such forego the poet's sacred name,
> Who rack their brains for lucre, not for fame:
> Still for stern Mammon may they toil in vain!
> And sadly gaze on Gold they cannot gain!
> Such be their meed, such still the just reward
> Of prostituted Muse and hireling bard!

For this we spurn Apollo's venal son,
And bid a long 'good night to Marmion.'
                                (11. 171-84)

Scott responded angrily to this charge in a letter to Southey:

> In the meantime, it is funny enough to see a whelp of a young Lord Byron
> abusing me, of whose circumstances he knows nothing, for endeavouring
> to scratch out a living with my pen. God help the bear, if, having little else
> to eat, he must not even suck his own paws. I can assure the noble imp of
> fame it is not my fault that I was not born to a park and 5000 a-year, as it
> is not his lordship's merit, although it may be his great good fortune, that
> he was not born to live by his literary talents or success. [25]

But while Byron's attack on Scott's motives may have been unfair, it is
evident that he still regarded him as a potentially great poet, as we see in
this passage showing the whole complex of Byron's feeling for Scott and
Scotland:

> But Thou, with powers that mock the aid of praise,
> Should'st leave to humbler Bards ignoble lays:
> Thy country's voice, the voice of all the Nine,
> Demand a hallowed harp—that harp is thine.
> Say! will not Caledonia's annals yield
> The glorious record of some nobler field,
> Than the vile foray of a plundering clan,
> Whose proudest deeds disgrace the name of man?
> Or Marmion's acts of darkness, fitter food
> For SHERWOOD's outlaw tales of ROBIN HOOD?
> Scotland! still proudly claim thy native Bard,
> And be thy praise his first, his best reward!
> Yet not with thee alone his name should live,
> But own the vast renown a world can give;
> Be known, perchance, when Albion is no more,
> And tell the tale of what she was before;
> To future times her faded fame recall,
> And save her glory, though his country fall.
>                                 (11. 931-48)

Byron thus indicated his faith in Scott's as yet unfulfilled potential, and
his high regard for what Scotland had been in ages past (but was not in an
age of Scotch Reviewers).    But Byron's vision now transcended
provincialism in arguing that a writer could move from being Scottish to
being British (telling the tale of Albion) and finally to being world-
renowned.    Clearly, he was preparing himself for his own career, which

had already carried him away from Scotland to an English schooling and now found him on the verge of travels in the Mediterranean. His Scottish identity was not to any point at this time; instead, Byron spoke for all Britain:

> For me, who, thus unasked, have dared to tell
> My country, what her sons should know too well,
> Zeal for her honour bade me here engage
> The host of idiots that infest her age;
> No just applause her honoured name shall lose,
> As first in freedom, dearest to the Muse.
> Oh! would thy bards but emulate thy fame,
> And rise more worthy, Albion, of thy name!
> (11. 991-98)

Byron was even capable of writing vicious anti-Scottish diatribe just before returning from the Mediterranean (in *The Curse of Minerva*).[26] But this was to prove the last time he let himself be upset over anything Scottish. Already in his travels he had viewed some scenes filtered through his own memories of Scotland and through Scott's verse.[27] Even more significant was the paradoxical effect of *Bards*, alluded to above: because Byron had attacked Scott, he had begun a relationship with Scott which was to result, after reconciliation of these early differences, in friendship. That friendship, in turn, was to bolster Byron's re-identification with Scotland.

It was Byron who, through the graces of John Murray, made the first step towards Scott.[28] A cordial correspondence followed, in which Byron apologized for *Bards*, explaining that 'The Satire was written when I was very young and very angry, and fully bent on displaying my wrath and my wit, and now I am haunted by the ghosts of my wholesale assertions.'[29] This correspondence culminated in the meeting at Murray's discussed above. Byron and Scott saw each other over a period of two months thereafter. The friendship which had begun with correspondence was carried on through it after Byron left England in 1816.[30]

Scott had begun even by the time of the 1815 meeting to represent more to Byron than a Scottish verse romancer: in 1814 he was the author of *Waverley*, and Byron was aware of his authorship within the year.[31] That novel seems to have had a profound effect upon Byron. It revived thoughts of Scottish life for him:

> *Waverley* is the best and most interesting novel I have redde since—I don't know when. Besides, it is all easy to me, because I have been in Scotland

so much (though then young enough too), and feel at home with the
people, Lowland and Gael.[32]

One account of Byron's conversation at this time indicates indeed how
extensive and emotionally involved were his thoughts of Scotland. Isaac
Nathan reports that during his period of acquaintance with Byron, circa.
1814-15, Byron discussed the writers, music, warriors, history, and clergy
of Scotland.[33] He regretted his inability to read Ramsay in dialect, but had
the highest praise for Burns. More revealing comments on other topics
had as theme the integrity of the Scottish people. Byron argued, for
example, that Scottish music was not so indebted to the Italians as some
had supposed, an important matter 'for the honour of the country.' The
Scottish clergyman 'is quite independent in the performance of his duties,'
unlike the hierarchical English clergy. Scottish education had higher
standards of qualification for its masters than the English.

What most captured Byron's imagination on the matter of Scottish
integrity was the history of her national struggles for independence, a
history of which he seemed to have a quite detailed knowledge. For
Byron, Scottish history was a record of great leaders—Wallace, Bruce,
Knox, the Pretender—fighting against oppressive English rule, and being
served sometimes quite faithfully by their people, but sometimes not,
when power had corrupted allegiance. Nathan observed of the first case,
that no one in all of Scotland was base enough to betray the Pretender for a
huge reward; Byron agreed that the fact 'draws forth the highest
encomiums on the national character, and was one fine specimen of the
retreat of avarice at the approach of integrity.' But Byron was especially
incensed by examples of betrayal. Of that of Wallace by the Scot
Monteith, he observed that 'even at this distant period, the deeds of the
father are visited upon the descendants, who are often reproached with the
barter of their country, in the part taken by their ancestors....' Most
horrible of all in the record of Scottish self-betrayal, Byron found, was the
1692 Massacre of Glenco (where Campbells acting as agents of the
English government massacred clan Macdonald):

> That deed, [said his Lordship], stamps the Conqueror with more infamy
> than any atrocity of savage barbarity. Only think for a moment, an ancient
> clan exterminated in a few hours: a family enjoying every comfort, and
> kindly entertaining a supposed friend with all that hospitality so peculiar to
> the Scotch: the soldiers quartered upon their tenants, and in the midst of
> festivity, the troops are ordered to fall upon the unsuspecting family, and
> in cold blood put every living thing to the sword. The carnage did not
> cease, when the stillness of death reigned at the mansion, but the whole

valley of Glenco was laid waste, by the merciless hand of a traitor, armed
with unrestricted power from a merciless monarch.

When Byron had finished this story, Nathan noted his extreme emotion:

> Lord Byron's feelings were here strongly excited—he clenched his fist—
> knitted his brow, and grinding his teeth, appeared in great agitation:
> several moments passed before he recovered his usual composure.

Byron's deep involvement in this story suggests how much his characteristic
hatred of tyranny could be aroused by awareness of the injustices inflicted
upon Scotland. It is no wonder then that *Waverley* with its story of the '45
and subsequent Waverley novels about other crises in Scottish history
were such potent experiences for him.

　　Without exaggeration one can say that from their inception, Byron was
a fanatical reader of the Waverley novels.  In his conversations, letters,
and *Journal*, Byron praised Scott's novels unstintingly and continuously:
'As a prose writer he has no rival; and has not been approached, since
Cervantes, in depicting manners. His tales are my constant companions,'
he told Pryse Gordon Lockhart in 1816.[34] He claimed in his *Diary* for 5
January 1821 that 'I have read all W. Scott's novels at least fifty times.'[35]
Byron told Medwin that 'I never travel without Scott's Novels; they are a
library in themselves—a perfect literary treasure. I could read them one a-
year with new pleasure.'[36]　Even with Byron's reduced baggage at
Cephalonia, Scott's novels 'were always scattered about his rooms.'[37] IIis
letters to Murray are filled with anxious questions about and entreaties to
send the latest Scott novel, even to the point of producing this amusing
juxtaposition which suggests that a Scott novel was for Byron a necessity
of life: 'Send me some soda-powders. some of "Acton's Corn-rubbers."
and W. Scott's romances.'[38]

　　There were several reasons for Byron's obsession with the Waverley
novels.  For one thing. Byronic hero-types abound, to the point where
Byron's sister and aunt thought he must have written some of the novels.[39]
But this point is better taken up below. Most important, both for the
discussion of Byron's sense of his Scottishness and for a demonstration of
those concerns which preoccupied him in exile and to his death, is the
Scottish matter of the Waverleys.  This matter dramatized two areas of
greatest concern for Byron: his Scottish backgrounds in ancestry and
boyhood, and wars of national liberation.

　　Byron in his continental 'exile' must have been naturally attracted to
the dominant plot convention of most of the Waverleys, that of the missing
or neglected rightful heir who is restored to his inheritance and honor.
Byron had sold Newstead Abbey in 1817, but his good name in Britain

had very few buyers at this time—in fact, he was to return only vicariously, through Don Juan.

The return the Waverleys offered was a deeper, psychological one to his own boyhood.  Byron wrote Scott in 1822 that 'to me those novels have so much of "Auld lang syne" (I was bred a canny Scot till ten years old),' and added, quoting from *The Heart of Mid-Lothian* (Ch. xlix),

> my 'heart warms to the tartan' or to anything of Scotland, which reminds me of Aberdeen and other parts, not so far from the Highlands as that town, about Invercauld and Braemar, where I was sent to drink goat's *fey* in 1795-6....[40]

One aspect of 'auld lang syne' was recollections of his ancestry roused in Byron by *The Abbot* (1820). The work is set in the time of Queen Mary, when Catholic Scots were trying to restore her to the throne.  Byron recounted  in much detail to Murray an ancestor's participation, as he remembered the account of it:

> *The Abbot* will have a more than ordinary interest for me; for an ancestor of mine by the mother's side, Sir J. Gordon of Gight, the handsomest of his day, died on a Scaffold at Aberdeen for his loyalty to Mary, of whom he was an imputed paramour as well as her relation. His fate was much commented on in the Chronicles of the times. If I mistake not, he had something to do with her escape from Loch Leven, or with her captivity there. But this you will know better than I.
>
> I recollect Loch Leven as it were but yesterday: I saw it in my way to England in 1798, being then ten years of age. My Mother (who was as haughty as Lucifer with her descent from the Stuarts, and her right line, from the *old Gordons, not* the *Seyton Gordons*, as she disdainfully termed the Ducal branch,) told me the Story, always reminding me how superior *her* Gordons were to the Southron Byrons, notwithstanding our Norman, and always direct masculine descent, which has never lapsed into a femalet as my mother's Gordons had done in her own person.[41]

This passage is revealing not only for the gossipy detailed interest shown by Byron but for the significant mistakes of memory which, nine days later, he wrote to Murray that he had made.  Byron had apparently checked an historical source and found among other matters that John Gordon

> suffered, *not* for his loyalty, but in an insurrection. He had *nothing* to do with Loch Leven, having been dead some time at the period of the Queen's confinement. And...I am not sure that he was the Queen's paramour or no...

I must have made all these mistakes in recollecting my Mother's account of the matter, although she was more accurate than I am, being precise upon points of genealogy, like all the Aristocratical Scotch.[42]

Byron's mistakes reveal a pattern of self-projection into John Gordon: handsome, loyal to an underdog, a lover, and the lover of a blood-relation. Thus was Byron imaginatively entering into the life of his own forbears.

In the last few years of his life, Byron reversed thoroughly and explicitly the public stance he had taken toward Scotland in the time of *Bards*. Speaking of fighting in Spain, he tells Douglas Kinnaird there will be 'some *fechting* as we Scottish say.'[43] In *Don Juan*, his narrator pays a tribute to Francis Jeffrey (whose *Edinburgh* had pilloried the young Byron, as we have seen, but whose own criticism thereafter was quite fair and judicious toward Byron), offers 'a Health to 'Auld Lang Syne,' and gives this famous reminiscence in Canto X:

17

And when I use the phrase of 'Auld Lang Syne!'
  'Tis not addressed to you—the more's the pity
For me, for I would rather take my wine
  With you, than aught (save Scott) in your proud city.
But somehow,—it may seem a schoolboy's whine,
  And yet I seek not to be grand nor witty—
But I am half a Scot by birth, and bred
A whole one, and my heart flies to my he

18

As 'Auld Lang Syne' brings Scotland, one and all,
  Scotch plaids, Scotch snoods, the blue hills, and clear streams,
The Dee, the Don, Balgounie's brig's black wall,
  All my boy feelings, all my gentler dreams
Of what I *then* dreamt, clothed in their own pall,
  Like Banquo's offspring;—floating past me seems
My childhood, in this childishness of mine:
  I care not—'tis a glimpse of *Auld Lang Syne*.'

19

And though, as you remember, in a fit
  Of wrath and rhyme, when juvenile and curly,
I railed at Scots to show my wrath and wit,
  Which must be owned was sensitive and surly,
Yet 'tis in vain such sallies to permit,
  They cannot quench young feelings fresh and early:
I '*scotched* not killed' the Scotchman in my blood,
  And love the land of 'mountain and of flood.'

Thus Byron reaffirms the 'Hours' Scottish poems as sincere ('it may seem
a schoolboy's whine. . . But I am half a Scot'). The enduring centrality
and importance of the early Scottish experience is also asserted in his last
long poem, *The Island*. Speaking of the young Scottish sailor Torquil and
his native bride, Neuha, Byron argues for the formative nature of
childhood experience:

> Both nourished amidst Nature's native scenes,
> Loved to the last, whatever intervenes
> Between us and our Childhood's sympathy,
> Which still reverts to what first caught the eye.
> He who first met the Highlands' swelling blue
> Will love each peak that shows a kindred hue,
> Hail in each crag a friend's familiar face,
> And clasp the mountain in his Mind's embrace.
> Long have I roamed through lands which are not mine,
> Adored the Alp, and loved the Apennine,
> Revered Parnassus, and beheld the steep
> Jove's Ida and Olympus crown the deep:
> But 'twas not all long ages' lore, nor all
> *Their* nature held me in their thrilling thrall;
> The infant rapture still survived the boy,
> And Loch-na-gar with Ida looked o'er Troy,
> Mixed Celtic memories with the Phrygian mount,
> And Highland linns with Castalie's clear fount.
> Forgive me, Homer's universal shade!
> Forgive me, Phoebus! that my fancy strayed;
> The North and Nature taught me to adore
> Your scenes sublime, from those beloved before.
>                                          (II.12. 276-97)

If foreign settings stirred memories of Scotland in Byron, so did the
literary and political fight for liberation—a fight which led finally to his
own death—take on the coloring of Scott's novels. By 1819 the Scots
idiom of those novels, especially where they deal with warfare, had
entered Byron's correspondence and journal. His own *Don Juan* he saw
figuratively as leading to civil war:

> I am particularly aware that *Don Juan* must set us all by the ears; but that
> is my concern, and my beginning: there will be *Edinburgh* and all too
> against it, so that, like Rob Roy, I shall have my hands full.[44]

Shortly after, Byron, now in Ravenna, was involved in a literal
insurrection (of Italian nationalists fighting the Austrian occupation). He

talked of defending the Pope, then by implication identified himself with Bucklaw, the reckless bandit in *The Bride of Lammermoor*, by calling a visitor 'Captain Craigengelt,' Bucklaw's associate:

> for I must 'boot and saddle,' as my Captain Craigengelt (an officer in the old Napoleon Italian army) is in waiting.[45]

Like Andrew Fairservice watching the Highlanders revolt in *Rob Roy*, Byron watched the Italian war developing:

> At last, 'The kiln's in a low.' The Germans are ordered to march, and Italy is, for the ten thousandth time to become a field of battle.[46]

When the Neapolitans commenced hostilities, Byron quoted from *Old Mortality* (Ch. v):

> in a short time 'There will be news O'thae craws,' as Mrs. Alison Wilson says of Jenny Blana's 'unco cockernony' in the *Tales of My Landlord*.[47]

And when Murray considered coming to Ravenna at this time, Byron wryly asserted in terms from *Waverley* (Ch. xviii).

> I will exercise the rites of hospitality while you live. and bury you handsomely (though not in holy ground), if you get 'shot or slashed in a creagh or splore.' which are rather frequent here of late among the native parties.[48]

The Waverleys did not serve merely to color Byron's language in this last period of his life. In a sense they were primers both for his own artistic rendering of historical crisis and for his own participation in such crisis. Committing himself to the Greek war of independence, Byron expressed himself in terms from *Waverley* and *Old Mortality*: 'At any rate, I shall cast in my lot with the puir Hill Folk!'[49] The surgeon on the ship which carried Byron to Cephalonia thought he had a Scottish accent, and Moore states that while on the island, Byron wore chiefly a Gordon tartan jacket.[50] And one might note that the day before leaving for Missolonghi. Byron shut himself away from officers and friends to read *Quentin Durward*, just received.[51] At his death. Byron seems to have felt he had that same 'ill-starr'd,' fated quality of the old Highland chieftains: he recalled that a fortune teller in Scotland had told him as a boy to beware his thirty-seventh year.[52]

The charting of Byron's attitudes to Scotland reveals a definite pattern of early affection for the land and its warrior tradition, a subsequent covering-over but not loss of affection in response to critical ridicule of it, a deliberate cosmopolitanizing of his sense of nationality, but finally, through his love of Scott and his novels, a reidentification with the early Scottish background. Byron's Scottish associations with his final Greek adventure would seem a silly sort of play-acting were it not for the depth of those associations as he came to see them.  There was no question of any current Scottish nationalism, as Byron was reconciled to the 1707 Union of England and Scotland.[53] Committing himself first to Italian and then to Greek independence, Byron apparently felt that his commitment had a prior origin in his boyhood admiration of Scottish fighters for freedom. His manner of leadership, pragmatic and unillusioned, even makes Byron resemble Edward Waverley (of *Waverley*) or Henry Morton (of *Old Mortality*), who like Byron tried in vain to discipline mobs into efficient military forces.[54]

The sureness of his *Don Juan* style and the realism of the work, and the desire to participate directly in the fight against tyranny, are part of that same process by which Byron embraced the memory and values of his Scottish boyhood, while moving into engagement with history.

# Notes

[1] *BLJ*. There is also a famous painting of this meeting, in the John Murray Collection, but it is an imagined view by one C.Werner from the 1850's. However, it makes a point: sitting are Isaac D'Israeli, John Murray II, Sir John Barrow, George Canning, and J.W. Croker. Standing off to the side by the window, conferring with each other as if in a world apart, are Byron and Scott. See also the editor's discussion of the meeting in Andrew Nicholson, ed., *The Letters of John Murray to Lord Byron* {Liverpool: Liverpool Univ. Press, 207), n.5, p.133-134. The Currier & Ives image is much more fanciful but likewise symbolic of the study which follows.

[2] Recounted in Thomas More, *Life of Lord Byron*, 1830.

[3] B*LJ*, 3, 219 (24 Nov. 1813).

[4] B*LJ*, 3, 250 (15 March 1814).

[5] John Gibson Lockhart, Memoirs, of the Life of Sir Walter Scott, *Bart.*, Author's Edition, 10 vols., 1839 (Edinburgh: Black, 1871), Ch. lxxxii.

[6] B*LJ*, 4, 146 (to Murray, 24 July 1814).

[7] Ernest J. Lovell, Jr., ed., *Medwin's Conversations of Lord Byron* (Princeton: Princeton Univ. Press, 1968), p. 137.

[8] *Life*. Ch. xxxvii.

[9] *The Author of Waverley*, pp. 18-19.

[10] H. J. C. Grierson, ed., *The Letters of Sir Walter Scott*. 12 vols. (London: Constable, 1932), III, 373. Hereafter, *Letters*.

[11] In letters of 3 Aug. 1814 to Murray and Moore, Byron notes that Scott is reportedly ill at ease on stormy seas, and deprecates such 'home-keeping bards' or 'home-keeping minstrels' (*BLJ*. 4, 151-2).

[12] *BLJ*, 9, 30. (*Detached Thoughts*. 15 Oct. 1821).

[13] Indicative of their shared sense of humor is a short piece by Scott in 1817 in what has come to be known as Byron's *Don Juan* manner. See Appendix B.

[14] An exception is Moray McLaren, *Sir Walter Scott: The Man and Patriot* (London: Heinemann, 1970), who calls the relationship 'a friendship compounded of affection and admiration, between two generous men whom the world thought different, but who had so much in common. . .,' p. 96.

[15] The book ostensibly devoted to the subject is Angus Calder, ed., *Byron and Scotland: Radical or Dandy?* (Edinburgh: Edinburgh Univ. Press, 1989), explores various byways around the topic, often through a lens of Scottish nationalism. Note, too, that while I have previously published on 'Byron and the Scottish Literary Tradition' (*Studies in Scottish Literature*, Columbia, SC: Univ. of South Carolina Press, 1979), this was intended as a useful critical tool but not an ascription of some mystical Scottish essence to Byron: he was a Scot and a Brit and an Internationalist; to be sure, Scotland came to be seen as important in his life, but it served his ongoing endeavors. The series of national identities Byron assumed are charted, as well as the fading out, then in, of his understanding of his Scottish Gordon background, in Bernard Beatty, 'The Force of Celtic Memories in Byron's Thought,' *English Romanticism and the Celtic World*, ed. Gerard Carruthers and Alan Rawes (Cambridge: Cambridge U.P., 2003).

[16] *Letters*, III, 140 (16 July 1812).

[17] The text for quotations from Byron's Poetry is J.J.McGann, Lord Byron: The *Complete Poetical Works* (Oxford: Oxford U.P, 1980-93).

[18] Thomas Moore, *Life of Lord Byron: With His Letters and Journals*, 6 vols. (1830; new edition, London: John Murray, 1854), I, 22; II, 36.

[19] Leslie Marchand, *Byron: A Biography* (New York: Knopf, 1957), I, 34.

[20] *The Island*, note for II, 291.

[21] To Elizabeth Bridget Pigot, 11 Aug. 1807, *BLJ*, 1, 132.

[22] Henry P. Brougham, unsigned review, *Edinburgh Review*, XI (February 1808), 285-89. A 'pibroch' is a tune, not an instrument. Byron corrected this misusage in *Childe Harold*, III.26.

[23] John Murray, ed., *Lord Byron's Correspondence*, 2 vols. (London: John Murray, 1922), I, 2 (to Hobhouse, 27 Feb. 1808). Hereafter, *LBC*.

[24] Mayne, *Byron*, 2 vols. (New York: Scribner's, 1912), I, 23; *Life*, I, 35-36.

[25] *Letters*, II, 214 (7 Aug. 1809).

[26] Byron was perhaps following a convention: Claude Fuess finds an analogue for the anti-Scottish verses of *Curse* in Churchill's *Prophecy of Famine* (1763), *Lord Byron as a Satirist in Verse* (1912; rpt. New York: Russell, 1964), pp. 88-89.

[27] *BLJ*, 1, 227 (to his mother, 12 Nov. 1809).

[28] Andrew Rutherford explores this dynamic in 'Byron, Soctt and Scotland,' in Charles E. Robinson, ed., *Lord Byron and His Contemporaries* (Newark: Univ. of

Delaware, 1982).  Also see John Clubbe in 'Bryon and Scott,' *Texas Studies in Literature and Language* (Spring, 1973).

[29] Prothero, Rowland E., ed. *The Works of Lord Byron: Letters and Journals.* 7 vols. (London: John Murrary, 1898-1901).  Account of the first step is at II, 131-35; on *Bards, BLJ*, 2, 182-83.

[30] There were to be wonderful surprises for Byron.  At a time when his name was reviled in Britain, an anonymous reviewer in *The Quarterly Review*, January 1816, praised *Childe Harold III*, refusing to mingle 'the faults of genius with its talents.' Byron wrote Murray, 3 March 1817, to express his extreme gratitude for and praise of the review: 'he must be a gallant as well as a good man, who ventured in that place, at this time—to write such an article even anonymously' (*BLJ*, 5,178).

Medwin noted of Byron that 'Perhaps of all his friends Sir Walter Scott had the most influence over him.  The sight of his hand-writing, he said, put him in spirits for the day.'  *Medwin's Conversations of Lord Byron*, ed. Ernest J. Lovell, Jr. (Princeton: Princeton Univ. Press, 1966), note, p. 268.

[31] Comment to Isaac Nathan, made in 1814, cited below, n. 32.  Scott did not publicly divulge his authorship of any novel before 1827.

[32] *BLJ*, 4, 146 (to Murray, 24 July 1814).

[33] Nathan was associated with Byron during the latter half of 1814 and of 1815, and for a few days before Byron left England in 1816. See Ernest J. Lovell, Jr., ed., *His Very Self and Voice: Collected Conversations of Lord Byron* (New York: Macmillan, 1954), p. xx. The material discussed here is 'Of Uncertain Date,' pp. 143-46.  Also worth noting at this point is that the 1816 Sale Catalogue of Byron's library showed Scottish poetry well represented. Elizabeth F. Boyd, *Byron's Don Juan: A Critical Study* (1945; rpt. New York: Humanities Press, 1958), p. 91.

[34] Lovell, *His Very Self*, p. 180.

[35] *BLJ*, 8, 13. He revised this number to 'forty times' in his 1 March 1821 letter to Murray, *BLJ*, 8, 88.

[36] Medwin's *Conversations*, p. 199.

[37] See John Murray, Jr., in *LJ* (Charles Hancock letter to Henry Muir, 1 June 1824).

[38] *BLJ*, 8, 121 (19 May 1821). See Appendix A for a list of the novels Byron reports having read.

[39] Explained in Byron's letter to Murray, *BLJ*, 5, 220 (9 May 1817).

[40] *BLJ*, 9, 86-87 (12 Jan. 1822 with 27 Jan. postscript, p. 6).

[41] *BLJ*, 7, 204 (16 Aug. 1820).

[42] *BLJ*, 7, 212 (25 Aug. 1820).

[43] *LBC*, II, 141 (14 April 1820).

[44] *BLJ*, 6, 123 (to Murray, 6 May 1819).

[45] *BLJ*, 7, 61 (to Murray, 9 March 1820).

[46] *BLJ*, 8, 43 (*Diary*, 5 Feb. 1821).

[47] *BLJ*, 8, 46 (*Diary*, 18 Feb. 1821).

[48] *BLJ*, 8, 74 (2 Feb. 1821).

[49] *BLJ*, 11, 82 (to Charles F. Barry, 24 Oct. 1823).

[50] Marchand, *Byron*, III, 1168; Moore. Life. I,35.

[51] *BLJ*,[6, 428.] Appendix VI (Hancock to Muir. 1 June 1824).

[52] Marchand, *Byron*, III, 1212.

[53] In his 'Address Intended to be Recited at the Caledonian Meeting' of 1814 (not published until 1830), Byron had memorably written:

O'er Gael and Saxon mingling banners shine,

And, England add their stubborn strength to thine.

The blood which flow'd with Wallace flows as free,

But now 'tis only shed for fame and thee.

(ll.9-12)

[54] See Fiona MacCarthy's account of the end in Missilonghi, where Byron's sense of realism (p. 494) and "practical humility" (p. 509) are extolled. *Byron: Life and Legend* (New York: Farrar, Strauss and Giroux, 2002).

# CHAPTER TWO

# THE USE OF HISTORY IN THE EARLIER WORKS OF SCOTT AND BYRON

...I hate things all fiction....There should always be some foundation of fact for the most airy fabric, and pure invention is but the talent of a liar.
—Byron to Murray, 2 April 1817

Scott's influence on Byron and his work seems assured from the evidence given above of background affinities and of Byron's extreme enthusiasm for and continued reading of the Waverley novels. However, it would be presumptuous and, indeed, implausible to interpret the development of Byron's poetry from 1814—the year *Waverley* was published—solely or even largely in the light of Scott's novels. As Elizabeth Boyd has said, 'Byron's mind was autocratic and incapable of receiving a single decisive influence.'[1] If superior to any one influence, Byron was on the other hand open to a great many at every turn in his writing, as Boyd's own study of his *Belesenheit* shows so well. To concentrate on the Waverley novels as influences accordingly requires an isolating focus, defined by the particular formal and thematic concerns represented by those novels. I would argue that Scott's novels dealt with crucial problems which confronted Byron in his personal and literary development and so provide a useful context in which to understand that development.

My procedure will be to demonstrate that Scott and then Byron, both greatly aware from the start of the record of man's past, his history, moved in their presentation of fictional hero-figures from an emphasis solely on the peculiarities of character to a more holistic view of human life, one that takes account of the conditioning forces of events and institutions. The difference in perspective is roughly that defined by Erik Erikson when he argued against the excessively subjectivist bias of modern psychology:

> We cannot even begin to encompass the human life cycle without learning to account for the fact that a human being under observation has grown stage by stage into a social world; this world, always for worse *and* for better, has step by step prepared for him an outer reality made up of

human traditions and institutions which utilize and thus nourish his developing capacities, attract and modulate his drives, respond to and delimit his fears and phantasies, and assign to him a position in life appropriate to his psychological powers. We cannot even begin to encompass a human being without indicating for each of the stages of his life cycle the framework of social influences and of traditional institutions which determine his perspectives. . . .[2]

It is, finally, their sharing of such an approach as this to human life which brings Byron and Scott together and sets them apart from the other major Romantics. I take this perspective to be the one Karl Kroeber called, in reference to Scott, the 'apprehension of life as historical process,' and I place its artistic products within the general category of historical fictions.[3] In Scott's early verse romances we find the development of an historical perspective which is increasingly functional artistically; this development provides an instructive parallel to that in Byron's work after 1814.

In Scott's earliest verse romance, *The Lay of the Last Minstrel* (1805), stock medieval romance elements—knights, a wizard, and a dwarf—predominate. 'History' provides no more than atmospheric details in a work which Scott said partook of 'the rudeness of the old Ballad, or Metrical Romance.'[4] In *Marmion* (1808), Scott introduces an actual historical event and character—the battle of Flodden Field and King James IV—and by presenting the great clash of the kingdoms of Scotland and England, arrives at the subject matter of his novels, the depiction of civilization in collision. Even so, the historical setting is only incidental to the romance of Marmion and Constance and of DeWilton and Clare: 'Mine is a tale of Flodden Field, / And not a history' (V.xxxiv.1013-14). On the other hand, the romantic tale of Malcolm Graeme and Ellen Douglas in Scott's next work, *The Lady of the Lake* (1810), is of little interest: Scott admitted that his fictitious Malcolm Graeme was a failure.[5] The vitality of the work derives from the great representatives of the clashing civilizations, Roderick Dhu and King James IV, and their struggle to the death. But here again the historical tale is not integrated with the romantic. *Rokeby* (1812) was Scott's last notable verse romance and, although unsuccessful because of its convoluted plot, is significant in the story of his development. Here at last Scott attempted to make his romantic story one with the historical. The struggle between Oswald and Bertram is integrated with the factionalism of the English Civil War and affected by the battle of Marston Moor: 'public event affects private experience,' as is necessary for any work in which history is artistically functional.[6]

Accompanying this change in the ordering of narrative priorities is an increasingly complex treatment of hero types. Sir William Deloraine of *Lay*, 'A stark moss-trooping Scot' (I.xxi.215), is pure ballad outlaw. Marmion, however, mingles his higher qualities (of a knight) with the particularly ignoble qualities of a forger (a trait Byron scorned in *English Bards*; 'Not quite a felon, yet but half a knight'—but which, Edgar Johnson observes, is historically authentic).[7] Roderick in *Lady* is a dark hero pitted against the equally strong fair one, James, and both are historically representative. Thus Scott qualifies his outlaw hero's autonomy as Byron does not do with his early Oriental Tale heroes but comes to do in later works. Finally, in *Rokeby,* there is a profusion of types—the Gothic Villain, Oswald; the Man of Feeling, Wilfrid; the Child of Nature, Redmond; and two Noble Outlaws, Mortham and Bertram. Scott's emphasis is, then, not upon the monolithic hero, but upon the context of social relationships and historically significant narrative into which these types fit, a key difference from Byron's early Oriental Tales.

Scott's art had now developed to the point where he could write truly historical fictions, in which history is not merely atmosphere or incidental adjunct, but is artistically functional. The time was opportune for Scott to pursue this line, for by 1814 Byron had outdone him in exoticism with his Oriental Tales. Verse was unsuitable for the detailed presentation of historical materials which Scott wished to make, and so he turned to prose and the novel, with the sensational results remarked upon by Byron.

Scott's presentation of historical crisis, his depiction of the individual facing that crisis, and the modal direction of his novels (toward comic resolution or tragic catastrophe) are matters to be treated in detail in the following chapters (Chs. THREE-FIVE). At this point it is important to take note of Byron's literary development before and after the advent of *Waverley,* for we shall see how after that novel he moves toward the depiction of his heroes in a significant historical context.

Byron produced two important groups of verse after *English Bards* and before reading *Waverley* and meeting Scott: the first two Cantos of *Childe Harold* (published in 1812), and four Oriental Tales—*The Giaour* and *The Bride of Abydos* (publ. 1813), *The Corsair* and *Lara* (publ. 1814). Both groups differ in an important way from the works which followed the year 1814, in that the heroes—constituting that complex known as the Byronic Hero—are relatively fixed in their characteristics and undergo little change: they are end-products of previous experience and stand, monumentally and colorfully, as types.

In Cantos I and II of *Childe Harold.* Harold is the sated refugee from 'Sin's long labyrinth' (I.5), and takes his jaded self on a tour of the

Mediterranean. But this tour is no process of change for him. Instead, it is the occasion for presenting to us history's end-product, the degenerate modern world. Portugal is squalid, Spain brutal, Greece a sad relic, and Albania barbarous. The tone of these early cantos is mournful and elegiac; the speaker is disenchanted with a present which does not measure up to the glories of the past.

In the Oriental Tales, the romantic love relation is the basis of the plot, as in Scott's earlier verse romances: there are the affairs of the Giaour and Leila, of Selim and Zuleika, of the Corsair and Medora, and of Lara and the mysterious Kaled. All these affairs are fated for the worst: Leila is killed and the Giaour lives on in remorse; Selim is killed and Zuleika dies of a broken heart; Medora kills herself and the Corsair goes on in grief with Gulnare who hopelessly loves him; as Lara, the Corsair dies in battle and Kaled (Gulnare) goes mad. The interest of these tales derives in part from these melodramatic plots but primarily from the exotic heroes of intense inward life.

The heroes of the Oriental Tales are similar to Harold in having arrived at a fixed state of mind. While they may be physically active (so is Harold as traveller)—the Giaour 'thundering comes on blackest steed' (1. 180)— they are 'psychically monolithic and inert.'[8] Each is the type of the man of mystery, harboring some guilt which sets him off from other men. The Giaour's visage is 'scathed by fiery Passion's brunt' (1. 195), and he is accused of having an 'inward hell' (1. 754); Selim's 'keen eye shone / With thoughts that long in darkness dwelt' (Bride. I.12.329-30); Conrad is 'That man of loneliness and mystery' (Corsair, I.8.173) whose 'dark eyebrow shades a glance of fire' (1.9.196); and Lara is 'a stranger in this breathing world' (I.18.315) bearing his mysterious burden of guilt (for the death of Medora, one presumes). Only insofar as Byron takes an interest in other characters—Giaffir in *Bride,* the suffering females—is there the possibility of moving away from the hero, outcast of humanity, to the hero, member of (and thus conditioned by) a social grouping.

It has been argued that *Lara* is a significant departure from the earlier tales in that 'Lara is not so much an outcast from humanity . . . as an outcast from one segment of a particular society.'[9] Indeed, Lara is the proudest member of a group of barons whom he despises, and consents to be the leader of a popular revolt—a theme Byron develops in greater depth in *Marino Faliero* (Ch.THREE below). But *Lara* still falls short of being an historical fiction. Kroeber gives as reason that Byron's choice to make time and place indefinite—'the country is not Spain, but the Moon,' Byron wrote[10]—'renders this interpenetration of the personal and the social virtually meaningless.' Yet, if such an interpenetration did occur in Lara, only the narrowest conception of 'history' would deny that the work is a meaningful model, at least, for historical fiction. The problem with Lara, indeed with all of these Tales and *Childe Harold*, is not their lack of historical or factual specificity—Byron from his earliest works was like Scott in scrupulously annotating particular points of history or custom. Rather, it is that the 'interpenetration of the personal and the social' fails in all of them, thereby nullifying them as historical fictions, because the heroes cannot escape the confines of self. In the midst of the serfs' revolt, for example, Lara is still set apart:

> And cared he for the freedom of the crowd?
> He raised the humble but to bend the proud.
> He had hoped quiet in his sullen lair,
> But Man and Destiny beset him there. . . .
> (II.9.897-900)

The Byronic Hero's lack of commitment to social life and affairs has given us our greatest monument of Romantic individualism but also gave Byron, I submit, a problem: the Byronic Hero is at odds with Byron's own tendencies as a self-styled 'man of the world.' There is, of course, no law requiring that an author's hero reflect himself, and Byron was the first to scorn the public's identification of himself with his heroes. But that an author's art is isolated from his own existential concerns and vision seems equally implausible, especially in Byron's case. The evidence of Byron's life and works is that he ultimately abandoned a supra-historical, aloof stance. That he ultimately did not accept withdrawal from the world as authentic for his life or his characters is the point toward which any study of his development should move.

With this approach, we can now see a problem raised by the Oriental Tale heroes which cries for solution. Their authority is supposed to derive from 'The power of Thought—the magic of the Mind!' (*Corsair*, I.8.182). But as one critic asks of Conrad, 'don't his career and his vaguely desolate end, to say nothing of Medora's, betray the liability of the mind to the harsh play of circumstances?'[11] in other words, Byron, in depicting heroes who forsake the world but are defeated by it, failed to recognize the context in which heroic action might prove authentic. Set attitudes about the state of human life were not enough for Byron or his heroes. Both needed to move to an understanding of life as process, however disastrous that process might prove to be. For Byron, as for Scott, process came to be understood in terms of history.

Byron's reading of *Waverley* and his meeting in 1815 with the man who had realized life as historical process in that novel was of great importance in his dealing with the problem evident in his own work and life. Byron did begin to experiment with forthrightly historical materials in the 1815-19 period, although the problem of the Byronic Hero's sovereign mind was not yet settled. His works in these years show us the ferment which led to his most significant exercises in historical fiction— the historical dramas, *Don Juan*, and *The Island*.

That Byron was now actively experimenting in the historical mode is revealed by a group of anecdotal tales produced at this time: *The Siege of Corinth* (written in early 1815), *The Prisoner of Chillon* (June 1816), and later *The Lament of Tasso* (written April 1817), *Mazeppa* (published in 1819), and *The Prophecy of Dante* (written in June 1819).[12] The change from the previous Tales is well exemplified in *Siege*, whose hero, 'Alp, the Adrian renegade' (3.114) is, like previous heroes, an exile, but for political reasons, not for some vaguely universal transgression: Alp is accused of being a traitor to his native Venice. His renegade status derives from his serving the Turks in their siege of Venetian-controlled Corinth. As a result of this precisely defined conflict of loyalties, Alp is a more believable and complete character than the previous heroes. As one student of Byron's tales has noted of the treatment of Alp, 'Like his prede-cessors he is alienated, outlawed, and separated from his lady-love, but here we are taken more into his feelings and psychology as he struggles with a moral dilemma.'[13] Thus we see Alp reflecting on the contrast between his situation and that of those who served in the old Spartan-Persian conflicts (several such examples from history are given in *Siege)*,

> . . . the glorious dead
> Who there in better cause had bled,
> He felt how faint and feebly dim
> The fame that would accrue to him
> Who cheered the band and waved the sword,
> A traitor in a turbaned horde;
> And led them to the lawless siege,
> Whose best success were sacrilege.
>                 (15. 394-401)

Byron has created a character of greater historical and moral definition than before, and allows history to pass judgment upon him: Alp's treacherous service in an unjust cause leads to a holocaust of defender and attacker wherein Corinth is 'lost and won' (33.1079). Byron is now critical of such a hero as we see from his sympathy for Corinth's defenders whom he describes in imagery reminiscent of Scott's for the beleaguered Scots in *Marmion*: Corinth's defenders, 'Like the avalanche's snow,' are washed down by 'the spring-tides' of Turks (24.743, 739), just as the

Scots before the English 'melted from the field, as snow, / When streams are swoln and southwards flow' (VI.24.1050-51).

In the other four anecdotal tales, both person and place are historically specific (only the historical setting of *Siege* is). Since they are monologues, they do not depict processes of historical change as a plotted narrative would. However, these tales are significant for both their historical bases and their reversal of the early tales' depiction of physically active but psychically static character-types; instead, they show with psychological nicety the mind's adjustment to the force of circumstance, be it through resistance (Tasso and Dante) or accommodation (Bonnivard and Mazeppa). The difference between the two groups of poems is significant: Tasso and Dante, as artists, can triumph over present adversity posthumously, through their art; Bonnivard and Mazeppa, a political activist and a soldier, must reconcile themselves to their present situations. Byron's distinction between men of letters and of action reveals his concern over the different options for his own life.

The emphasis on the force of circumstance is shown best in *The Prisoner of Chillon*. In the tale, we find a careful account of the effect of imprisonment on Francois de Bonnivard, held in the Chateau de Chillon on Lake Leman from 1532 to 1536. Rather than dealing with the 'Eternal Spirit of the chainless Mind!' celebrated by the Sonnet to Chillon the moral of the tale treats of accommodation to chains:

My very chains and I grew friends,
So much a long communion tends
To make us what we are....
                (11. 389-91)[14]

In all these anecdotal tales, Byron has carefully depicted the mind in process of adjustment to a variety of circumstances of historical significance. The more he pays attention to such circumstances, the more Byron moves from melodrama to historical fiction. *Beppo* (1818), a forerunner of *Don Juan* in style, shows Byron's new willingness to examine with more care the objective social conditions within which his hero moves. Byron's critical self-awareness has reached the point where he can poke fun at his earlier tales: a writer seeking an easier task than *Beppo*, his narrator says, would 'sell you, mixed with western Sentimentalism, / Some samples of the finest Orientalism' (LI). Beppo's career as a renegade is distanced, and we see him involved in a highly sophisticated, complex social world, a. kind of Involvement discussed in the treatment of *Don Juan* below (Ch. FOUR).

Two major works, *Manfred* and *Childe Harold* III and IV, show that Byron still faces two ways: toward poetic protest against the metaphysical injustices of the human condition and toward the need for active participation in the historical process. In *Manfred* (1817), Byron applies to the Byronic Hero of the mind his new method of detailed characterization but without any significant historical setting. The setting is in Faustian Gothic, and *Manfred* is an attempt—in fulfillment of the Sonnet on Chillon and 'Prometheus'—to depict a chainless mind. The price of Manfred's autonomy is, however, an apparently final darkness. Byron has used his defiant hero to protest man's metaphysical condition; but, for a Byron not personally prepared to waste away in death, Manfred's gesture of death could be no existentially viable response to the human predicament. One critic sees the work as a catharsis for Byron:

> By finding in *Manfred* the perfect artistic expression for his experiences, Byron achieved an emotional release, a separation from his hero which freed him to develop the larger view of himself and the world in which the hero became increasingly unnecessary, even a little silly.

That Byron was free of 'his hero' is untrue, and the fact is not explained by describing later uses of the Byronic Hero type as 'interludes within the greater drama of *Don Juan*.'[15] While *Don Juan* does depict a hero immersed in historical process, it does not depict or resolve the problem of the deeply willful hero. The immersion of the willful, Byronic Hero in historical process is the task Byron set himself in the Historical Dramas (Ch. THREE below).

One must agree, though, that Byron developed a 'larger view of himself and the world.' The last two cantos of *Childe Harold* show, especially by their contrast with the earlier cantos, how comprehensive his outlook had become. In them, the narrator increasingly usurps the gloomy Harold's place as the central experiencer, until in Canto IV (completed in January 1818), he jettisons Harold altogether and begins to come to terms with the meaning of historical process and his own relation to it. As Joseph writes, the central theme of 'time and mortality and of lament for lost empires . . . is now given a new and more specifically historical dimension by Byron's reading of Gibbons,' where he could see the conception of the evolution of empires.[16] True, the poet still sees history as a cyclical pattern of decline from high aspiration and promise into disaster:

> There is the moral of all human tales;
> 'tis but the same rehearsal of the past,
> First Freedom, and then Glory—when that fails,
> Wealth—Vice—Corruption,—Barbarism at last.

> And History, with all her volumes vast,
> Hath but *one* page. . . .
> (IV.108)

But he has discovered a resource of the self, 'that within me which shall tire / Torture and Time, and breathe when I expire' (IV,137), adequate in its persistence to respond to the persistent destructiveness of history. And he has discovered Freedom and Glory, enduring values worth exerting himself for and allowing him to leave behind what one critic calls the 'earlier Childe-ish jadedness or apathy':[17]

> Yet, Freedom! yet thy banner, torn, but flying, Streams like the thunder-storm *against* the wind; Thy trumpet voice, though broken now and dying, The loudest still the tempest leaves behind. . . .
> (IV.98)

Freedom is a seed 'Sown deep' which 'a better spring' shall bring forth, even if it grows only 'less bitter Fruit' (98). As Jerome McGann has observed, this last qualification is no affirmation of political apocalypse.[18]

It is, however, sufficient basis on which to go forward into the process of human life. The end of Byron's psychological pilgrimage in *Childe Harold,* with its clear-eyed recognition of the evil and occasional good in life, is also the beginning of an existentially committed pilgrimage.

It is now that one can appreciate the pertinence of the world of Scott's novels. We have seen how Byron in 1819 thought of his participation in the Italian fight for freedom in their idiom. In his writing, too, there is a turn from the suprahistorical Harolds, Conrads, and Manfreds to heroes who participate or attempt to participate in the ongoing flow of human life, man's history. Three Historical Dramas contemplate the varieties of heroism within historical crisis and move to the concept of a viable hero; at last, Don Juan travels through various countries of modern Europe and, in the manner of a Waverley Hero, takes part in great events. Since *Don Juan* spans the last six years of Byron's life, I turn first to the examination of the dramas written in 1819-21.

# Notes

[1] *Byron's Don Juan* (1945; rpt. New York: Humanities Press, 1958), p. 159.

[2] *Young Man Luther: A Study in Psychoanalysis and History (*New York: W. W. Norton, 1958), p. 20.

[3] *Romantic Narrative Art* (Madison: Univ. of Wisconsin Press, 1960), p. 169.

[4] All quotations from Scott's poetry use Horace E. Scudder, ed., *The Complete Poetical Works of Sir Walter Scott* (Boston: Houghton Mifflin, 1900).

[5] *Letters* . II, 464 (to Miss Smith, 12 March 1811).

[6] Kroeber, p. 176

[7] *Sir Walter Scott: The Great Unknown,* 2 vols. (New York: Macmillan, 1970), I, 345.

[8] Kroeber, p. 144.

[9] Kroeber, p. 142.

[10] *BLJ*, 4, 146 (to Murray, 24 July 1814).

[11] M. G. Cooke, *The Blind Man Traces the Circle: On the Patterns and Philosophy of Byron's Poetry* (Princeton: Princeton Univ. Press, 1969), p. 85.

[12] *Parisina* was published with *Siege* and, while based on an incident in Gibbon's writings, is a melodramatic account of incest and has little in common with the other anecdotes.   It seems to belong to an earlier period than the historical anecdotes and, indeed, according to Byron's note, was begun before *Lara* (Poetry. Ill, 507-08, n. 3).

[13] Robert D. Hume, 'The *Island* and the Evolution of Byron's Tales,' in W. Paul Elledge and Richard L. Hoffman, eds., *Romantic and Victorian; Studies in Memory of William H. Marshall* (Rutherford, N.J.: Fairleigh Dickinson Univ. Press, 1971), p. 162.

[14] The Sonnet is in the same vein as 'Prometheus' (also 1816); the issues involved in both short poems are dramatically realized in *Manfred* (1817), discussed below.

[15] Edward E. Bostetter, Introduction, George Gordon. *Lord Byron; Selected Works,* 2nd ed. (New York: Holt, 1972), xix.

[16] M. K. Joseph, *Byron the Poet* (London: Gallancz, 1964), p. 94; also Boyd, *Byron's Don Juan*, p. 104.

[17] Cooke. *The Blind Man*, p. 123.

[18] Jerome J. McGann, *Fiery Dust: Byron's Poetic Development* (Chicago: Univ. of Chicago Press, 1968), p. 133.

# CHAPTER THREE

# THE INDIVIDUAL IN HISTORICAL CRISIS: *OLD MORTALITY* AND THE HISTORICAL DRAMAS

> Human nature can best be studied in the state of conflict; and human
> conflict comes to the detailed attention of interested recorders mainly
> under special circumstances. One such circumstance . . . is history. . .
> —Erikson, *Young Man Luther*

In the Historical Dramas—*Marino Faliero. Sardnaapalus*, and *The Two Foscari*—the Byronic Hero, like the typical Waverley Hero, faces the ordeal of historical crisis. Both authors realize that such crises have their own remorseless dynamics, subjecting the individual to processes which pose a fearful threat to the humane principles held in the best of times. The way each author depicts that crisis and his hero's participation in it is the concern of this chapter. Two works, *Old Mortality* and *Marino Faliero,* will be examined to begin with, in considerable detail, to show the issues involved.

Although written for the most part in 1820 and published in 1821, *Marino Faliero* was initially conceived in 1817, at the same time Byron was writing the historical anecdotes and the final canto of *Childe Harold.* Samuel Chew gives some of the aesthetic reasons for Byron's turn to the historical drama (as a reaction against the extravagance of the current English stage which Byron had observed in his Drury Lane tenure):

> From the horrible he reacted to the heroic, from medieval and exotic
> settings to historical, from utter lack of truth to nature to insistence upon
> fact, from unrestrained wildness to an almost austere control, from
> outworn and often unhealthy harpings upon love to study of the problems
> of states.[1]

To these reasons can be added the encouraging example of the *Waverley* novels. Neither in the anecdotal tales nor in *Childe Harold* had Byron had the scope for presenting the complex interplay of motives and forces in historical crisis which is the substance of the *Waverley* novels. The drama did afford greater scope. For reasons which are not clear, however, Byron set *Marino Faliero* aside until 1820, when perhaps his own involvement with the revolutionary Carbonari hastened his resolve to deal with the precise intricacies of a fourteenth-century conspiracy to overthrow a city-state: like the Doge Faliero, Byron found himself, an aristocrat, dedicated to the overthrow of a government.

*Waverley* had been an account of revolution, the abortive Jacobite '45. But by 1820, Scott had produced other accounts of civil struggle—including *Rob Roy*, *A Legend of Montrose*, *Ivanhoe*, *The Monastery*, and *The Abbot*—the most pertinent of which, in relation to *Marino Faliero*, is *Old Mortality* (1816). There are more than thematic reasons for choosing this novel for comparison.

Byron first reported reading it in May 1817—the period in which he was conceiving the play.[2] In early 1820, when he produced a translation of Pulci's *Morgante Maggiore*, Byron wrote in the Advertisement of Scott's 'exquisite use of his Covenanters in the *Tales of My Landlord*,' a reference to *Old Mortality*. Therefore the novel had been in his mind in 1817 and was still so when Byron in the spring of 1820 continued and finished *Marino Faliero*.

The different modes and genres of the works rule out an exact comparison; and each work expresses a different attitude to the result of historical development, but this is a matter for comment in Chapter V. Our concern here is to show the similar treatment by both works of the individual's involvement in historical crisis: (1) a moment of such crisis, the collision of social forces, has arrived; the opposing factions are delineated, and the hero is critical of both. However, (2) the hero suffers private wrongs whose source he locates in public vices; for redress, he must enter the crisis, and there he establishes his moral identity.

## (1) The Structure of Historical Crisis

*Old Mortality* and *Marino Faliero* both depict insurrections against an established government. In each case, the dialectic of opposing factions allows inhumane forces full play.

*Old Mortality* is set in the Scotland of 1679, and deals with the armed rising of the Covenanters, extreme Presbyterians who demand the restoration of the Solemn League and Covenant of 1643 which carried with it freedom of worship from the English church and allowed Scotland a relatively republican form of government. Socially, the Covenanters are a lower-class, peasant group. The government they oppose (that of

Charles II) seeks to restore upper-class control. The resulting struggle is thus drawn along religious and social lines.

Scott establishes the perilousness of the historical atmosphere by having characters repeatedly comment on the strangeness of the times in explanation of the brutality and unlawful behavior of soldiers in the struggle. His explanation of the lawlessness is that

> in times of civil discord . . . the highest qualities, perverted by party spirit, and inflamed by habitual opposition, are too often combined with vices and excesses which deprive them at once of their merit and of their lustre. (Ch. ii, p. 131)[3]

His hero, the middle-class Henry Morton, stands initially aloof from the struggle, for he perceives the inhumanity of both sides:

> the reasons of neutrality which he had hitherto professed had root in very different and most praiseworthy motives. He had formed few congenial ties with those who were the objects of persecution, and was disgusted alike by their narrow-minded and selfish party-spirit, their gloomy fanaticism, their abhorrent condemnation of all elegant studies or innocent exercises, and the envenomed rancour of their political hatred. But his mind was still more revolted by the tyrannical arid oppressive conduct of the Government—the misrule, license, and brutality of the soldiery—the executions on the scaffold, the slaughters in the open field, the free quarters and exactions imposed by military law, which placed the lives and fortunes of a free people on a level with Asiatic slaves. (Ch. xii, p. 142)

This description of the opposing forces is fully illustrated in the characters of their leaders. The Covenanters' principal leader is Burley Balfour, a monomaniac of elemental vitality:

> one in whom some strong o'ermastering principle has overwhelmed all other passions and feelings, like the swell of a high spring-tide, when the usual cliffs and breakers vanish from the eye. (Ch. v, p. 62)

Burley in his religious zeal is a self-appointed agent of God's will, taking vengeance on those he regards as evil. He opposes Morton's belief in fully constituted authority;

> Is not punishment justly inflicted, whether on the scaffold or the moor? And where constituted judges, from cowardice, or from having cast in their lot with transgressors, suffer them not only to pass at liberty through the land, but to sit in the high places, and dye their garments in the blood of the saints,—is it not well done in any brave spirits in the public who shall draw their swords in the private cause? (Ch. xx. 216)

The issue here is not between mundane and supra-mundane law. Morton believes in both a higher law of humanity and a mundane due process of law:

> That the Almighty, in his mysterious providence, may bring a bloody man to an end deservedly bloody, does not vindicate those who, without authority of any kind, take upon themselves to be the instruments of execution, and presume to call themselves the executors of divine vengeance. (Ch. xx, p. 216)

Burley violates both concepts of law, disregarding due process in the name of a higher but inhumane law of wrath. Accordingly, we see him assassinate an archbishop and lead the merciless slaughter of royalist forces. He takes inspiration from what Morton calls 'the mingled ravings of madness and atrocity' (Ch. xxii, p. 223), the Old Testament wrath of Habakkuk Mucklewrath:

> . . . who speaks of mercy to the bloody house of the malignants? I say take the infants and dash them against the stones — take the daughters and the mothers of the house, and hurl them from the battlements of their trust, that the dogs may fatten on their blood. . . . (Ch. xxi, p. 223)

Morton's earlier fear proves to be well founded:

> who shall warrant me that these people, rendered wild by persecution, would not, in the hour of victory, be as cruel and as intolerant as those by whom they are now hunted down? (Ch. v, p. 67)

The leader of the royalist side, the dashing cavalryman Claverhouse, is cut from the same cloth as Burley:

> a spirit unbounded in daring and in aspiring, yet cautious and prudent as that of Machiavel himself. Profound in politics, and imbued, of course, with that disregard for individual rights which its intrigues usually generate, this leader was cool and collected in danger, fierce and ardent in pursuing success, careless of facing death himself, and ruthless in inflicting it upon others. (Ch. xi, p. 131)

As a result, he gets no more sympathy from Morton than Burley did. Morton observes that the orders Claverhouse issues,

> for life and death, the securing of his prisoners, and the washing of his charger's shoulder,—were given in the same unmoved and equable voice, of which no accent or tone intimated that the speaker considered one direction as of more importance than another. (Ch. xxxiii, p. 322)

Not only does Claverhouse disregard the law of humanity-, but like Burley he bends existing laws to his purposes: when told no law seems appropriate for the prosecution of a particular recusant, he says, 'I think I could find one' (Ch. xi, p. 132). Claverhouse attempts to distinguish 'between the fanaticism of honour and that of dark and sullen superstition,' but Morton sees only that 'you both shed blood without mercy or remorse' (Ch. xxxiv, p. 327).

Each leader thus feels that his cause justifies all means necessary for its advancement. Basic human rights are crushed between the colliding factions. For an observer, such as Morton at first is, the struggle is a madness, conducted by madmen. But even he must become involved, as we shall see.

*Marino Faliero*, a drama, must arrange its materials differently from a novel. Therefore, instead of carefully reviewing the buildup of opposing factions as a novel can afford to do, the opening scene concerns the event which finally impels the hero to participate in historical crisis, and the overall crisis becomes clear only subsequently. Nevertheless, for purposes of comparison we adhere to the format used so far for *Old Mortality*.

*Marino Faliero* is set in fourteenth-century Venice, and deals with the conspiracy of its Doge and a group of plebeians to overthrow the ruling patrician oligarchy, the Forty. This oligarchy has become increasingly oppressive toward the plebeians. Thus the struggle is drawn along social lines.

The Doge Faliero, like Morton, has stood aloof from the unrest of the lower classes. In all his service to Venice, he recalls that 'not for any knot of men, / Nor sect, nor faction, did I bleed or sweat!' (I. ii.467-68) . The Doge sees upper and lower classes as contemptible, as is clear in his comment on a slander against his own honor,

> . . . Left a base slur to pass from mouth to mouth
> Of loose mechanics, with all coarse foul comments,
> And villainous jests, and blasphemies obscene;
> While sneering nobles, in more polished guise,
> Whisper'd the tale, and smiled upon the lie
> Which made me look like them....
> (I.ii.189-94)

Once the conspiracy to overthrow the patricians is in progress, the issue of dehumanizing fanaticism is raised. The leader of the lower-class faction, Israel Bertuccio, is as monomaniacal as Burley:

We must forget all feelings save the one;
We must resign all passions save our purpose. . . .
(II.ii.600-01)

Another conspirator states that purpose: the patricians form 'one mass, one breath, one body. . . . So let them die as one' (III.ii.155, 158). The Doge, wavering before adhering to this extremism, observes that the conspirators '*feel* not—*you* go to this butcher-work / As if these highborn men were steers for shambles' (III.ii.627-28). In joining with the extremists, however, he reveals the same Old Testament wrath as a Habakkuk Mucklewrath, with its dehumanization of the opposing factions:

The blood of tyrants is not human; they,
Like to incarnate Molochs, feed on ours. . . .
(IV.ii.512-13)

I cannot pause on individual hate,
In the absorbing, sweeping, whole revenge,
Which, like the sheeted fire from heaven, must blast
Without distinction, as it fell of yore,
Where the Dead Sea hath quenched two cities' ashes.
(III.ii.540-45)

But the Doge clearly sees the immorality forced upon men in crisis:

I will resign a crown, and make the state
Renew its freedom—but oh! by what means?
The noble end must justify them. . . .
Oh World!
Oh Men! what are ye, and our best designs,
That we must work by crime to punish crime?
(IV.ii.508-10, 514-15)

Lost in such a crisis is the relatively moderate voice of the one conspirator whose 'hesitating softness' (II.ii.581) is, as circumstances develop, dangerously weak and in fact the source of the conspiracy's failure:

I own my natural weakness, I have not
Yet learned to think of indiscriminate murder
Without some sense of shuddering; and the sight
Of blood which spouts through hoary scalps is not
To me a thing of triumph, nor the death
Of man surprised a glory. Well—too well
I know that we must do such things on those
whose acts have raised up such avengers; but

If there were some of these who could be saved
From out this sweeping fate, for our own sakes
And for our honour, to take off some stain
Of massacre which else pollutes it wholly, I had been glad. . . .
                                                (III.ii.185-97)

On the opposing side, the patrician Lioni shows himself capable of the same efficiency and single-mindedness counseled by the conspirators (but he is also a sympathetic figure, which raises problems to be discussed below in Chapter THREE).   On hearing of the conspiracy from his old friend Bertram, he moves without hesitation to arrest all conspirators, and they are soon executed.

Lioni's action allows one final point to be made about the ruthlessness of factions in the civil rebellion of both *Old Mortality* and *Marino Faliero;* no compromise is possible between them, and each must press to the absolute defeat of the other.   Morton attempts to deal with the English commander, the Duke of Monmouth, on behalf of the Covenanters, in hopes of arriving at a bloodless settlement of grievances.   He argues that rebellion has been pursued only as a last resort, and that to lay down arms would be to admit the invalidity of the rebel cause: until their rights are granted, the rebels cannot surrender. The Duke explains that 'I can only treat with supplicants, not with rebels' (Ch. xxix, p. 298), that is, that until the rebels surrender, no rights can be granted.   There is no resolution possible, then, except through war.

Likewise, once Faliero has set his own rebellion going, he knows that the only sanction of it lies in its success:

If we should fail, employing bloody means
And secret plot, although to a good end,
Still we are traitors. . . .
        (III.i.76-78)

Accordingly, the chief government spokesman declares that there is no treatment possible for Faliero except execution.

Historical crisis as pictured in these two works thus has its own remorseless dynamics, which allow inhumane elements to come to the fore, and force onlooking men of humane principles to examine their position carefully—and perhaps compromise it.  How the man of humane principles nevertheless becomes involved in such crisis is, then, the problem for both authors.

## (2) Private Wrongs from Public Vices

Because of his non-alignment with the factions dividing the kingdom, Henry Morton would simply 'have left Scotland, had it not been for his attachment to Edith Bellenden' (Ch. xii, p. 142). The Bellendens are an upper-class royalist family and disapprove of any match with Morton. Morton's attachment to Edith, and one other circumstance, a family debt to Burley Balfour, combine to implicate him in the perils of his time.

Morton repays his father's debt to Balfour by hiding him from pursuing royalists led by Claverhouse. When this is discovered, Morton is arrested. Even so, nothing might come of the matter if it were not for the attachment to Edith. While under custody at the Bellenden castle, Morton com^s to believe a rumor that Edith is really in love with Lord Evandale. It is no more than rumor, but Morton is an insecure young man, 'ingenious in tormenting himself,' and suddenly his state of arrest, heretofore irrelevant to his outlook on the crisis, becomes significant:

> 'And to what do I owe it,' he said, 'that I cannot stand up like a man, and plead my interest in her ere I am thus cheated out of it?—to what, but to the all-pervading and accursed tyranny, which afflicts at once our bodies, souls, estates, and affections! And is it to one of the pensioned cut-throats of this oppressive Government that I must yield my pretensions to Edith Bellenden?—! will not, by Heaven!—It is a just punishment on me for being dead to public wrongs, that they have visited me with their injuries in a point where they can be least brooked or borne.' (Ch. xii, p. 145)

Morton's personal sufferings thus become symbolic to him of the social grievances of the Covenanters. A few more provocations are enough to effect

> a singular and instantaneous revolution in his character. The depth of despair to which his lave and fortunes were reduced—the peril in which his life appeared to stand—the transference of Edith's affections . . . seemed to destroy every feeling for which he had hitherto lived, but at the same time awakened those which had hitherto been smothered by passions more gentle though more selfish. Desperate himself, he determined to support the right of his country, insulted in his person. (Ch. xii, p. 146)

Thus a sense of slighted personal honor and of unjust treatment by the established authorities catapult Morton from indifference to active involvement in the crisis of his time.

Like Morton, the Doge Faliero has for long had no reason to be disaffected with his government. He has held his post with honor and uneventfully. But a seemingly minor event proves decisive in changing his attitude. Steno, a member of the Forty, writes on the ducal throne a baseless slander on the fidelity of the Doge's wife. This slander, like the rumor which had so distressed Morton, strikes at the Doge's personal honor:

> . . . a poisonous libel,
> And on the honour of—oh God!—my wife,
> The nearest, dearest part of all men's honour. . .
> (I.ii.85-87)

The ruling Forty, however, see the offense as a piece of trivial mischief and put Steno under arrest for a month. The Doge expected a death penalty, so grievously had the matter upset him, and feels the Forty have betrayed him. Only now does he become fully interested in the injustices in the realm:

> I know the people to be discontented. . .
> Since they are nothing in the state. . . .
> (I.ii.326, 330)

He grants an interview to the plebeian Israel Bertuccio, who complains that a patrician dishonorably struck him over some trifling matter. The Doge now identifies his own dishonor with that the people suffer from the Forty: 'Our private wrongs have sprung from public vices' (III.ii.275).

We can see that Byron involves his hero in historical crisis in a manner similar to Scott's. Both writers have set themselves the problem of linking the personal passion of their hero with social-historical causes. But while both have used similar circumstances to spur the hero on into historical crisis, their handling of subsequent motivation and character development is quite different; indeed, Scott's handling is skillful and consistent, while Byron's is not.

A combination of circumstance and personal motivation led to Henry Morton's commitment to the Covenanters. While part of Morton's motivation is based on youthful self-doubt, on the erroneous belief that a Royalist is taking Edith from him, Scott has it that this is only *one* factor of many influencing Morton. Other factors include the inherited obligation to help Burley and the genuine grievances motivating the Covenanters. All factors combine to propel Morton into a new future and a new selfhood. Morton's own evaluation of these changes is worth quoting at length, for it illustrates Scott's thorough definition of Morton's changing outlook:

When Morton was left alone to his own reflections, with what a complication of feelings did he review the woods, banks, and fields, that had been familiar to him! His character, as well as his habits, thoughts, and occupations, had been entirely changed within the space of little more than a fortnight, and twenty days seemed to have done upon him the work of as many years. A mild, romantic, gentle-tempered youth, bred up in dependence, and stooping patiently to the control of a sordid and tyrannical relation, had suddenly, by the rod of oppression and the spur of injured feeling, been compelled to stand forth a leader of armed men, was earnestly engaged in affairs of a public nature, had friends to animate and enemies to contend with, and felt his individual fate bound up in that of a national insurrection and revolution. It seemed as if he had at once experienced a transition from the romantic dreams of youth to the labours and cares of active manhood. All that had formerly interested him was obliterated from his memory, excepting only his attachment to Edith; and even his love seemed to have assumed a character more manly and disinterested, as it had become mingled and contrasted with other duties and feelings. As he revolved the particulars of this sudden change, the circumstances in which it originated, and the possible consequences of his present career, the thrill of natural anxiety which passed along his mind was immediately banished by a glow of generous and high-spirited confidence.

'I shall fall young,' he said, 'if fall I must, my motives misconstrued, and my actions condemned, by those whose approbation is dearest to me. But the sword of liberty and patriotism is in ray hand, and I will neither fall meanly nor unavenged. They may expose my body, and gibbet ray limbs; but other days will come, when the sentence of infamy will recoil against those who may pronounce it; and that Heaven whose name is so often profaned during this unnatural war, will bear witness to the purity of the motives by which I have been guided.' (Ch. xxvi, p. 263)

Morton asserts the 'purity' of his motives: the personal motivation concerning Edith turns out to have been merely a catalyst for connecting Morton with the objective social forces of the time. Once committed to the struggle, Morton changes, and our evaluation of him must keep pace with the newness in and around him.

Morton's main characteristics are prudence and moderation. He is even less willing than Byron's Bertram to compromise means for ends, as we see in his retort to Burley: 'We are in arms to put down such cruelties, and not to imitate them' (Ch. xxvi, p. 267). Thus the Scott hero asserts humane law against the dehumanizing pressures of wartime expediency. But Morton's moderation, unlike Bertram's, is not presented as weakness. First of all, it is the product of great self-control, as symbolized by Morton's (albeit vain) attempt, as a military advisor, to instill principles of discipline into the Covenanting army. Second, it leads to a prudent *realpolitik,* for Morton leaves avenues of communication open to the royalist side, earns their respect, and is thereby able ultimately to survive the execution of his fellow leaders. The Scott hero is thus to be understood within the context of the comic resolution of most Waverley novels: he represents the ideal humanity which survives the nightmare of history.

The hero of *Marino Faliero*—indeed of all three of Byron's Historical Dramas—is presented in a tragic mode and does not survive the nightmare of history. Faliero has a flaw, like all tragic heroes, but his identity as a figure of stature inspiring our awe and pity is problematical, perhaps because of the peculiarities of the *historical* drama. With Scott's practice providing helpful contrasts, we can examine the key difficulty of *Marino Faliero.* the personal motivation of the hero.

Mindful of Faliero's extreme rage over the slander against his wife, Byron in his Preface draws from his knowledge of history to show how there can come 'so great an effect from so slight a cause.' He relates no fewer than thirteen examples from history: 'that a basin of water spilt on Mrs. Masham's gown deprived the Duke of Marlborough of his command, and led to the inglorious peace of Utrecht. . . . that Commodus, Domitian, and Caligula fell victims not to their public tyranny, but to private vengeance,' and so on. We should not be surprised, Byron argues,

> that a man used to command, who had served and swayed in the most important offices, should fiercely resent, in a fierce age, an unpunished affront, the grossest that can be offered to a man, be he prince or peasant. The age of Faliero is little to the purpose, unless to favour it—

> 'The young man's wrath is like straw on fire,
> *But like red hot steel is the old man's Ire.'*

Byron here justifies Faliero's rage on historical grounds as being in the spirit of the age, and on psychological grounds as part of the Lear-like nature of old men.

Within the drama, further plausibility is lent to Faliero's outrage over both Steno's slander and the Forty's failure to punish him severely when we find it shared by Israel Bertuccio:

> Is 't possible? a month's imprisonment!
> No more for Steno?
>            (I.ii.425-27)

> What! The same who dared
> To stain the ducal throne with those foul words,
> That have cried shame to every ear in Venice?
> (I.ii.417-19)

Bertuccio's agreement serves two purposes. First, as a spokesman for the people—there is no reason to believe he is simply trying to gain the Doge's favor—he shows that the Doge's anger is in the spirit of the times, and not to be greatly wondered at. Second, he reinforces the Doge's suspicion that the Forty are unjust and corrupt. Thus personal wrong may be seen as symbolic of social injustices. Byron has established the ingredients for a proper historical drama. Lukacs's formula for such drama is that

> the fruitfulness of a really dramatic theme depends on how deep the inner connection is between the persons at the centre of the drama and the concrete collision of the social-historical forces, i.e. on whether and in what way these characters are engaged with their whole personality in the conflict. If their tragic passion coincides at its heart with the decisive, social moment of the collision, then, but only then, can their personalities acquire a fully unfolded and rich, dramatic relief. The emptier, the more abstract and peripheral this relationship, the more must the dramatic hero undergo his development *alongside* the drama proper; that is from an artistic point of view.[4]

We have seen that Scott does not fail to make a deep interconnection between Henry Morton's personal motivation and the social problems of the day. The problem with *Marino Faliero* is that the connection between personal motivation and objective social causes, between the Doge's rage over the slight to his honor and the corruption of Venice's ruling class is not taken as the basis for a new selfhood for the Doge, but is, in fact, subverted. Byron never seems able to get beyond Faliero's wrath, even though he has made initially a good case for it, even though the plot does not call for it (the conspiracy fails because of Bertram's moderation, not the Doge's wrath), and even though the last act would profit from less emphasis on it. Let us see how Byron treats the Doge's passions.

Our sympathy for Faliero's rage begins to be undermined by the criticisms put forth by his wife, Angiolina. Since she is presented as a faultless character, her views of her husband are authoritative:

> His faults are those that dwell in the high bosoms
> Of men who have commanded; too much pride,
> And the deep passions fiercely fostered by
> The uses of patricians, and a life

Spent in the storms of state and war; and also
From the quick sense of honour, which becomes
A duty to a certain sign, a vice
When overstrain'd, and this I fear in him.
And then he has been rash from his youth upwards,
Yet tempered by redeeming nobleness. . . .
(II.i.103-12)

Our sympathy for Faliero's rage is further shaken in the scene immediately following this speech, when the conspirators (Faliero not present) make it clear that the issues of the crisis must and—for them—*do* transcend mere personal passion:

We will not strike for private wrongs alone;
Such are for selfish passions and rash men,
But are unworthy a Tyrannicide.
(II.ii.527-29)

This speech amounts to a gloss on Faliero's peripheral relation to the developing crisis. It does appear that he is striking 'for private wrongs alone'; in Lukacs's phrase, he has begun to develop '*alongside* the drama proper.'

The case against Faliero is made stronger, with some ambiguous qualification, by the manner of his participation in the climactic events of the conspiracy. There he must join in assassination attempts against patricians whom he has known personally. Faliero is depicted as more sensitive than his plebeian comrades, for he is horrified by the enormity of what must be done:

When all is over, you 'll be free and merry,
And calmly wash those hands incarnadine;
 But I, outgoing thee and all thy fellows
In this surpassing massacre, shall be,
Shall see and feel—oh God! oh God! 'tis true,
And thou dost well to answer that it was
'My own free will and act,' and yet you err,
For I *will* do this! Doubt not—fear not; I
Will be your most unmerciful accomplice!
And yet I act no more on my free will,
Nor my own feelings—both compel me back;
But there is *hell* within me and around,
And like the demon who believes and trembles
Must I abhor and do. Away! away!
(III.ii.629-42)

One expects to be able to find a tragic necessity here: the sensitive man embraces extreme means to overcome an even greater evil.  But, as described, Faliero's extreme actions are not to flow from a complex moral awareness: *that* is absorbed by his outrage over what is to be done.  The part of him that advances to the deed is unwilled, compelled by the vague '*hell* within . . . and around.'  It is therefore more a matter of helpless self-description rather than of consciously chosen decision when Faliero asserts that

> To me, then, these men have no *private* life,
> Nor claim to ties they have cut off from others;
> As Senators for arbitrary acts
> Amenable, I look on them—as such
> Let them be dealt upon.
>                    (III.ii.503-07)

Faliero is by his own testimony acting against his better judgment, for he knows the patricians do have private lives.  Byron decisively directs our sympathy away from Faliero at the outset of Act IV, by the long soliloquy revealing through its sensitivity and devotion to Venice, the sensuous beauty of the patrician Lioni's *private* life, exactly that aspect of the patricians which Faliero has described himself as ignoring.[5]  (And in the trial scene of Act V, he invests the patricians with dignity.)

With our sympathies for the patricians now aroused, and being filled with uncertainties about the validity of Faliero's position, we are prepared to watch the working out of Faliero's folly.  But in a later account of his own actions, although Faliero speaks in the self-justify ing idiom of Scott's Burley, he does make a case for the validity of the by then failed conspiracy:

> *Doge.*        It was ever thus
> With me; the hour of agitation came
> In the first glimmerings of a purpose, when
> Passion had too much room to sway; but in
> The hour of action I have stood as calm
> As were the dead who lay around me: this
> They knew who made me what I am, and trusted
> To the subduing power which I preserved
> Over my mood, when its first burst was spent.
> But they were not aware that there are things
> Which make revenge a virtue by reflection,
> And not an impulse of mere anger; though
> The laws sleep, justice wakes, and injured souls
> Oft do a public right with private wrong,

And justify their deeds unto themselves.—
                    (IV.ii.442-56)

The qualification '*oft* do a public right' shows Byron's uncertainty over how to evaluate Faliero's action. *Is* Faliero fighting for a public right by means of the 'private wrong' of killing men wholesale, or is he not? Byron's failure to handle Faliero's passionate nature consistently makes it impossible to answer the question.

In the first two scenes of the last act, the case appears complete against Faliero's passion. The government spokesman berates him for having a 'fury, like an angry boy's' (V.i.242). Faliero seems to agree, for he recalls his 'rash young anger' (V.ii.597) when years before he struck a bishop and received this curse:

> The Glory shall depart from out thy house,
> The Wisdom shall be shaken from thy soul,
> And in thy best maturity of mind
> A madness of the heart shall seize upon thee;
> Passion shall tear thee when all passions cease
> In other men, or mellow into virtues. . . .
>                    (V.ii.606-11)

It would seem finally that Byron has written off Faliero for his 'madness of the heart.' In terms of the plot, this is not a necessary conclusion. The conspiracy fails because of Bertram's humane moderateness, not because of Faliero's passion. Such a failure makes a good case for the tragic necessity of adopting extreme means. Thus Faliero's stature as a tragic hero would have been enhanced greatly if Byron had emphasized that the extremism he finally espouses was forced on him by the objective conditions of history. As it is, we are left uneasily with the feeling that subjective conditions have predominated in Faliero, that the social cause was only opportunistically seized upon to serve his private passions.

Of course, this interpretation is not one that Byron or any reader could be happy with, and so Byron goes through one final reversal of position to establish some connection between Faliero's personal motivation and objective historical significance. Before his execution, Faliero aspires to immortality and prophetic vision:

> I speak to Time, and to Eternity
> Of which I grow a portion, not to man.
> Ye Elements! in which to be resolved
> I hasten, let my voice be as a spirit upon you!
> . . . . . . . . . . . . . . . . . .

I am not innocent—but are these guiltless?
I perish, but not unavenged; far ages
Float up from the abyss of Time to be,
And show these eyes, before they close, the doom
Of this proud city, and I leave my curse
On her and hers for ever!
        (V.iii.722-26, 736-41)

Byron is finally trying to have it both ways: we have been presented with the personal tragedy of an old man, too passionate to be wise or morally admirable; on the other hand, he *is* wise and great, because he sees that the cause in which he enlisted was the right one and that its failure is historically momentous; he is given the moral authority to curse his opponents.

Such a contradiction at the center of *Marino Faliero* allows most commentators to dismiss the work as weak, or as a reflection of Byron's personal uncertainties. Viewed in the light of Scott's treatment of the individual in historical crisis, however, the problem in this play is aesthetically interesting and provides a revealing insight into Byron's literary development.

Byron has fallen into the classic dilemma of the historical writer, one which Lukacs praised Scott for avoiding: the dilemma of 'either romantically monumentalizing the important figures of history or dragging them down to the level of private, psychological trivia.'[6] Faliero is pinioned on both horns of the dilemma: Byron's emphasis on the private, psychological trivia of Faliero's passionate nature makes his hero's aspiration to significant action and vision inconsistent, so that the last scene is a bit of romantic monumentalization. Byron's need to write the last act, an act which Chew finds to be an 'undramatic aftermath'[7] and in violation of the strict principles of classical drama (because coming after the real catastrophe, the arrest of the conspirators in Act IV), may be ascribed to the necessity of salvaging Faliero's moral identity in the interests of an *historical* drama.

The following conclusions will help put the problem of *Marino Faliero* in perfective. This was Byron's first attempt at an historical fiction, and his eagerness to be true to the facts concerning Faliero's irascibility led to an unwise emphasis in the treatment of his personal motivation. As M. K. Joseph has observed of him, 'Once again the Byronic hero is a man who acts irrationally, swayed by "the madness of the heart."'[8] Byron had attempted a new genre, the historical tragedy, but made use of his old mode of characterizing the hero, perhaps in the ill-founded belief that the Byronic Hero was well suited to be tragically flawed. In illustrating the flaw, Byron may have been misled by Scott's emphasis on the evil of inhumane extremism into condemning his own hero to such an extent that recovery was impossible. Byron's earnestness in trying to achieve an historical drama is revealed by the last act. Faliero had to be raised from his own pathology of rage to be a figure of commanding moral stature and vision, of historical significance. His speech on the future decline of Venice reveals Byron's effort to meet the standard faced by what Lukacs has described as the true historical writer, the bringing of 'the past to life as the prehistory of the present.'[9]

*Marino Faliero* shows that little connection can be made between the profound self-involvement of the Byronic Hero and the objective social world. Perhaps Byron tried to avoid 'the madness of the heart' of this type of hero in his next historical drama, in creating the mild-mannered Sardanapalus; but the reversal of Faliero's character-type is only ironic. *Sardanapalus* depicts, like *Marino Faliero,* the ineffective attempt by a hero to make the transition from private to public life. However, some justification must first be given for treating *Sardanapalus* next after *Marino Faliero ,* for such is not the usual critical practice.

Samuel Chew's seminal study of the dramas established the view that *Sardanapalus* is 'the greatest' of them, while *The Two Foscari* is negligible, 'largely a reworking' of Faliero.[10] Most subsequent critics—including Joseph, Gleckner, Marchand, and McGann—have followed the practice of expediently neglecting *Foscari* by filing it away behind *Faliero* on the basis of their shared setting—'The Two Venetian Plays,' Chew called them—and of discussing *Sardanapalus* last as a kind of culmination.[11] Such an emphasis does violence to any reasonable account of literary development, for it ignores the fact that

*Sardanapalus* (January to May 1821) was written before *Foscari* (June and July 1821). Therefore, when Joseph, after acutely locating a division of values in *Foscari,* describes *Sardanapalus* as an 'attempt at reconciliation,' he gives the entirely false impression that Byron emerges from these plays with a fixed rather than an ambivalent attitude toward the problem of man's private and public lives.[12]

*Sardanapalus,* like *Faliero,* explores the relation between a ruler's private life and his public, historical role. Both plays show us leaders who act inappropriately—that is, without convincing moral authority—in historical crisis. This common theme is obscured in most critical discussions because of the relatively greater attractiveness of Sardanapalus and his views over Faliero and his. Byron has reversed outward character types so that instead of madness of the heart we have mildness; instead of rage, pacifism. When Sardanapalus expounds his pacifism, critics nod approvingly. Thus Chew introduces the play by saluting Byron's hostility to war as in 'The modern spirit of international understanding.'[13] Ironically, this judgment was expressed at the outset of World War I, but the irony can be appreciated only by realizing that ideas are not good or bad in themselves, but only insofar as they are appropriate to the circumstances of life. The appropriateness of Sardanapalus and his ideas to his position as king and to the circumstances of his times is the overriding problem in the play.

Considered in isolation from his historical context, Sardanapalus is an admirable creature. A philosopher aware of 'the fatal penalties imposed on life' (I.ii.354) in general—in this respect he is like Manfred or Cain, timeless and universal in his frame of reference—and of the hollowness of human glory, which is bought with the blood of conquest, Sardanapalus turns to Epicureanism. For his own life, he affirms love ('my life is love,' I.ii.406) and pleasure as absolutes: 'Eat, drink, and love; the rest's not worth a fillip' (I.ii.252). With fine fellow-feeling, he is sympathetic with and benevolent toward his subjects:

> . . . enough
> For me, if I can make my subjects feel
> The weight of human misery less, and glide
> Ungroaning to the tomb: I take no license
> Which I deny to them. We are all men.
>                                    (I.ii.309-13)

These are fine sentiments, but only in the abstract: they fail to take into account the competing human interests and ambitions which make for historical change. They are simply inappropriate, as we are reminded persistently by Sardanapalus' realistic brother-in-law Salemenes and by his favorite concubine, Myrrha. Salemenes continually wishes Sardanapalus would be 'that / Which he should be' (I.i.19-20), and accuses him of stopping 'Short of the duties of a king' (I.ii.408). Myrhha 'would not have him less than what he should be' (III.i.413). Both have a concept of the appropriate, Salemenes swearing 'I shall ever duly serve my sovereign' (II.i.518) and Myrhha speaking of 'due punishment' (II.i.575) to rebels. We find Sardanapalus toward the end admitting with self-pity in the same terms that 'I know not what I could have been, but feel / I am not what I should be' (IV.i.333-34).

The play's plot, too, ironically reverses that of *Faliero;* as Joseph puts it, 'whereas Faliero's violence leads him into conspiracy against the state, the mildness of Sardanapalus encourages conspiracy against himself.'[14]

Myrrha explains the weakness of his position.   The duty of a ruler, as she sees it, is to keep men

> …in awe and law,
> Yet not oppress'd—at least they must not think so;
> Or if they think so, deem it necessary,
> To ward off worse oppression, their own passions.
> (I.ii.585-87)

The wise ruler, then, must provide the restraint men need.   For Sardanapalus, this is reason for despairing of men:

> Oh, men! ye must be ruled with scythes, not sceptres,
> And mow'd down like the grass, else all we reap
>  Is rank abundance, and a rotten harvest
> Of discontents infecting the fair soil,
> Making a desert of fertility.
> (I.ii.461-65)

Thus Sardanapalus, like earlier Byronic Heroes, has a tendency to bewail the nature of man rather than to accept it and face up to the business of being one.   Worse, he will not act on this insight—'I'll think no more' (I.ii.466)—and even refuses to consider the guilt of two conspirators brought before him by Salemenes.   When the inevitable rebellion breaks out, Sardanapalus must finally, too late, take action.   He proves too rash a warrior (a revealing change in behavior), fighting 'like a young soldier' (IV.i.564).   When Salemenes prudently advises awaiting reinforcements before attacking, Sardanapalus reveals how carried away he is by battle:

> I detest that waiting. . . .
> My soul seems lukewarm; but when I set on them,
> Though they were piled on mountains, I would have
> A pluck at them, or perish in hot blood!—
> Let me then charge!
> (IV.i.556-57, 561-64)

Sardanapalus acts too quickly, with the result that Saleraenes is mortally wounded, and the king's forces lose.   The work ends in the manner of *All for Love* with Sardanapalus and Myrrha immolating themselves.[15]

Even this brief account of the action in *Sardanapalus* reveals that in essential outline the work is similar to *Faliero*.   In both, the hero enters the historical crisis confusedly, fails, and then aspires to apotheosis.   These matters bear closer examination.

Sardanapalus, like Faliero, faces a crisis in which there are two distinct factions. Further, they in fact resemble those in *Old Mortality;* on the rebel side, Beleses, a religious fanatic like Burley, ruthless in purpose; on the government side, a soldier of the king, Salemenes, as resolute as Claverhouse (though not, one feels, as unscrupulous). But as in *Faliero,* the supreme political figure must lend his support for the apparently just side to prevail. Sardanapalus eventual participation is as problematical as Faliero's. Again, personal motive does not move forward into public cause with any coherence. Sardanapalus opts first for an inappropriate mildness, then for an inappropriate, fatal rashness.

Sardanapalus' startlingly opposite responses to events derive not from any growth in character, but from confusion over his identity, as revealed in his nightmare (IV.i). The 'hunter' and the 'crone' of that dream corre-late with his earlier recollections of Nimrod, founder of the kingdom, and Semiramis, his 'wild grandam' (III.1.6) who sought to conquer other kingdoms. In his dream, Sardanapalus is horrified by Semiramis, but wishes to take the hand of Nimrod, who then vanishes. This subconscious urge toward achieving dynastic continuity clashes with Sardanapalus' conscious intention to break from the past. Consequently, we are left uncertain of the precise motivation and moral quality of his fight against the rebels. His rashness in battle bespeaks the same self-indulgence with which he had pursued pleasure.

If Sardanapalus' failure reminds us of Faliero's, his end partly resembles but points beyond, for Byron now seems clear about the nature of that failure. Sardanapalus has failed at involvement in the affairs of men, because he has been more involved in himself and his private life. It is appropriate that he die with his mistress 'All for Love': the parallel with another play allows us to recall, once more in Lukacs's terms, that the hero's, drama has in a sense developed alongside the historical drama proper. But where in *Faliero* Byron was inconsistent in his handling of Faliero's motivation, where he produced a catastrophe that owed nothing to Faliero's inner torment (Bertram was the betrayer), in *Sardanapalus* the hero's failure to escape the turmoils of the self is made the cause of the catastrophe.

Byron's more critical view of such a hero is evident in Sardanapalus' views on glory and heroism. Earlier in the play, Sardanapalus denies the historical significance of human action, scorning the achievements of great men:

> ...I dispense with
> The worship of dead men; feeling that I
> Am mortal, and believing that the race

From whence I sprung are—what I see them—ashes.
(II.i.239-42)

But at the end, mounted on his funeral pyre, Sardanapalus sees that his actions have been historically significant and will speak to the historical future:

> ...the light of this
> Most royal of funereal pyres shall be
> Not a mere pillar formed of cloud and flame,
> A beacon in the horizon for a day,
> And then a mount of ashes, but a light
> To lesson ages, rebel nations, and
> Voluptuous princes.  Time shall quench full many
> A people''s records, and a hero's acts;
> Sweep empire after empire, like this first.
> Of empires, into nothing; but even then
> Shall spare this deed of mine, and hold it up
> A problem few dare imitate, and none
> Despise—but , it may be, avoid the life
> Which led to such a consummation.
(V.i.436-53)

The lesson Sardanapalus would have the ages heed is partly admonitory, partly self-serving: voluptuous princes will learn greater responsibility, but Sardanapalus expects also to be admired for his unworldliness.  One critic accordingly finds that this suicide, 'even apart from its ostentation,' generates misgivings, for it smacks 'as much of egotistical chagrin as of unworldly self-abnegation.'[16]  Sardanapalus is properly regarded with this ambivalence because of his attempt to be historically significant while he fails from, and dies in glorification of, a privatistic ethic.  It is as if Byron had now articulated for himself the problem implicit in the aloofness of the Byronic Hero.  While he still treats Sardanapalus ambiguously, the lesson Byron is learning is to 'avoid the life / Which led to such a consummation.'

A more sympathetic reading than mine would declare, in the words of Joseph, that the tragedy of both Faliero and Sardanapalus is that 'they are defeated, not that they are wrong.'[17]  I have argued that there is so much personal inadequacy and suspect motivation in these heroes, that they *are* wrong, in terms of the concrete situations and issues they face.  Perhaps Byron had this wrongness in mind when he said that Sardanapalus is 'almost a comic character.'[18]  The only direction in which Byron could move at this point is toward a hero who renounces a privatistic ethic, and this he does in *The Two Foscari*.

*The Two Foscari* is Byron's first drama dealing forthrightly with heroic figures who have made the full commitment to public life. In the two preceding plays, such characters (Lioni and Salemenes) were minor, but their very commitment to contributing to the life of Venice and Assyria made the titular heroes seem only partially involved in the crises of history and more involved in themselves. *Foscari* deals, on the other hand, wholly with the varieties of commitment to a country (the city-state, Venice). The issues are now those which concerned Scott: the clash between the laws of the state and the laws of natural humanity.

*Two Foscari* is a revenge play: the Patrician Loredano, convinced that the Doge, Francis Foscari, was responsible for the death of his father and uncle, has conceived an undying hatred for the Doge. He intrigues to avenge himself by exploiting the laws of the state to the end that Francis and his son, Jacopo, will be disgraced and, in some way, exterminated. Jacopo has been in exile for crimes never clearly proven against him, but, at the play's opening, is brought back for torture and prosecution on a charge of treason. Apparently he has written a treasonous letter to the Duke of Milan; the truth seems to be that Jacopo contrived the letter not in order to betray Venice, but to cause himself to be brought back to the native land he loves so much, from which he cannot bear to be exiled. Because there is no legal proof of his innocence, the Doge must send him into exile once again. The sentenced Jacopo dies of a broken heart at the very moment of his departure. At the same time, Loredano, who had been instrumental in urging Jacopo's exile, leads a successful effort in the governing Council to force Francis into retirement by reason of age. His son dead, his identity as Doge stripped away, Francis dies of the accumulated shocks, and Loredano has taken his vengeance.

The keystone of the play, as can be seen, is Loredano. His determination to make the Foscari 'Extinct' (I.i.20) causes the moderate Senator Barbarigo to declare that Loredano is 'marble to retain / A feud' (IV. i. 323-24), and 'A very Ovid in the art of *hating*' (V.i.136). Loredano represents aspects of Faliero and Sardanapalus taken to an extreme: he uses the state to serve his personal ends. In this play, such a character is vilified as the source of the crisis itself. He is a type we meet repeatedly in Scott's novels, working through the law, considered abstractly and not humanely, to destroy enemies and achieve selfish ends: Gilbert Glossin in *The Antiquary* and Godfrey Bertram in *Guy Mannering* are two examples.

Two characters balance Loredano. Barbarigo is a moderate humanist, who criticizes Loredano but does so only as an observer. When Loredano asks of an unjust decree he rigidly supports, 'who shall oppose that law?' Barbarigo retorts, 'Humanity!' (IV.i.259). Loredano tells him it is too late to change the law now and to 'leave the rest to me' (V.i.264), and Barbarigo then turns to another line of thought.   The man of selfish passionate purpose is effective against the more disengaged moral *raisonneur*.

Responding to Loredano with more energy is Jacopo's wife, Marina, who berates him for his cruelty at every step.   She is a persistent critic of both husband and father-in-law.   As well (to anticipate for a moment the discussion below), hers is the loud affirmative voice of natural humanity, and she holds to a social contract theory in which a state may be disregarded if it be unjust to the individual:

> The country is the traitress, which thrusts forth
> Her best and bravest from her. . . .
> > (II.i.386-87)

> Accursed be the city where the laws
> Would stifle Nature's!
> > (II.i.419-20)

That older line of criticism which celebrates Byron's 'Eternal Spirit of the Chainless Mind' celebrates Marina's triumphant rejoinder to her imprisoned husband that 'The mind should make its own' liberty (III.i.84).[19]   But the weight of the entire play, the Two Foscari themselves, are testimony that such defiance is too simple, too disengaged, when set against the human life which in commitment accepts the suffering as well as the rewards.

The focus of *Two Foscari* is not upon Barbarigo or Marina and their arguments for absolute justice and freedom, but upon the two who have sacrificed much of their simple personal freedom for love of country, who have made an identification of their private and public lives.

Jacopo is, like Lioni, intoxicated with the sensuous aspects of his country:

> . . . the earth, and sky, the blue of ocean,
> The brightness of our city, and her domes,
> The mirth of her Piazza; even now
> Its merry hum of nations pierces here,
> Even here. . . .
> > (I.i.164-68)

Even in his dungeon, because it is a Venetian dungeon, Jacopo is happier than in exile, where he knows he would waste away.   When Marina preaches that the mind can make its own liberty, regardless of place, Jacopo retorts,

That has a noble sound; but 'tis a sound,
A music most impressive, but too transient:
The mind is much, but is not all.
(III.i.85-87)

What is all for Jacopo is love of country and of his fellows:

It is strength,
I say,—the parent of all honest feeling.
He who loves not his Country can love nothing.
(III.i.182-84)

I know if mind may bear us up, or no,
For I have such, and shown it before men;
It sinks in solitude: my soul is social.
(III.i.107-09)

Jacopo is the anti-type of the Byronic Hero: he has commitments to this life, to this history of this race of beings. He represents the soft, loving side of man, and conceives of his native land as being a mother: 'my native earth / Will take me as a mother to her arms' (I.i.142-43). The Doge Francis, by contrast, represents the severely dutiful side of man, and conceives of country as being a stern, law-giving father.

The Doge comes across as the character of greatest dignity and importance in the work. Byron wrote to Murray that 'What I seek to show in *The Foscaris* [sic] is the suppressed passions.'[20] Francis is Byron's hero of suppressed passion, having given over his life to the state: 'I have no repose; that is, none which shall cause / The loss of an hour's time to the State' (II.i.40-41). He knows his son is being tortured, but to the clamourous Marina's charge that he has abandoned Jacopo, he explains:

I shrank not from him:
But I have other duties than a father's;
The state would not dispense me from those duties. . . .
They must then be fulfill'd.
(II.i.183-85, 187)

Francis has eschewed the spontaneous promptings of 'nature,' such as animate Marina in, we now see, her over-simple way. He has accepted the rigor of service to the unnatural order of civilization. Marina calls Francis 'The stoic of the state' (IV.i.214), and he is, achieving through the private pain of self-control a greater, public good :

I have observed with veneration, like

A priest's for the high altar, even unto
The sacrifice of my own blood and quiet,
Safety, and all save honour, the decrees,
The health, the pride, and welfare of the State.
(II.i.255-59)

Stoicism, it may be noted here, was one quality Byron admired in Scott's characters: 'Both Byron and myself were much struck with the soliloquy of the fisherman to his boat, in which his son had been drowned,' said Cobhouse with reference to *The Antiquary*.[21] There Saunders Mucklebackit explains that while one child is drowned, four others remain to be fed. Pounding the boat's patched side, he gives this vignette of endurance:

Yet what needs ane be ongry at her, that has neither soul nor sense?— Mthough I am no that muckle better mysell. She's but a rickle o' auld rotten deals nailed thegither, and warped wi' the wind and the sea; and I am a dour carle, battered by foul weather at sea and land till I am maist as senseless as hersell. (Ch. xxxiv, p. 316)

Byron examined the shock of circumstance in *Chillon*. In *Two Foscari*, he finally gives us a hero who, like Mucklebackit, continues on nonetheless, with a stoical commitment to humanity carrying him past despair. It would be wrong to emphasize the Doge alone. He is balanced by his son's rich, emotional humanity. But in establishing *two* Foscari, Byron has posited a division, in the words of Joseph, 'between his desire for simple freedom and natural justice and his feeling that there is a necessary authority.'[22] The Doge's stoic stalwartness does finally yield, when his son dies and his retirement is forced upon him, to his feelings as a man and father, feelings which kill him. In a sense, the father becomes the son at last. But Byron does not accept the union in one person, as Scott does, of authority and humanity. The two principles are shown to be at odds, for the Doge's full acceptance of a position of authority required him to suppress his human feelings. However, that Byron could ennoble a hero of suppressed passions marks an immense change from an emphasis on man as self-assertive to man as self-regulative. The initially wavering, but finally firm, restrained hero of so many of Scott's novels enters Byron's work.

The two Foscari, then, unlike Faliero and Sardanapalus, are selflessly committed to love of country, each in his own way. Once again, however, they are defeated men; but the ongoing record of Byron's own activities in Italy and his last journey, to Greece, testify to his belief that historical crisis is worth participating in, whatever the odds. A step toward the literary presentation of the individual's survival of historical crisis was Scott's practice of using a modest hero and a more inclusive narrative form, and this is the line Byron had already begun to follow in *Don Juan*.

# Notes

[1] *The Dramas of Lord Byron* (Baltimore: Johns Hopkins Press, 1915), p. 36.
[2] *BLJ*. 5, 117 (to Murray, 9 May 1817).
[3] The text for all quotations from Scott's novels is *Waverley Novels,* ed. D. Laing, Centenary Edition, 25 vols. (Edinburgh: Black, 1870-71).
[4] Lukacs, *The Historical Novel,* p. 114.
[5] In 'A Political Interpretation of Byron's *Marino Faliero.*' *MLQ.* 3 (1942), 417-25, E. D. H. Johnson makes a case for Byron's own patrician loyalties. I am concerned in the present argument with the aesthetic implications of such biographical considerations.
[6] *Historical Novel*, p. 47.
[7] *Dramas*, p. 57.
[8] *Byron*, p. 114.
[9] *Historical Novel*, p. 53.
[10] *Dramas* pp. 105, 99.
[11] An exception to this practice is that of M. G. Cooke, who sees that *Foscari* 'runs a decidedly different course' from the two preceding dramas, *The Blind* Man, p. 183.
[12] *Byron*, p. 115.
[13] *Dramas,* p. 109.
[14] *Byron*, p. 116.
[15] M. G. Cooke explores the parallel with Dryden in 'The Restoration Ethos of Byron's Classical Plays,' *PMLA*, 79 (1964), 569-78.
[16] Cooke, *The Blind Man*, p. 73, n. 7.
[17] *Byron*, p. 116.
[18] *BLJ*. 8, 155 (to Murray, 22 July 1821).
[19] Cf. Chew, *Dramas,* pp. 102-03.
[20] *BLJ*, 8, 218 (20 Sept. 1821).
[21] Conversation of 8 Sept. 1816. Lovell, *His Very Self,* p. 194.
[22] *Byron*, p. 115.

# CHAPTER FOUR

# THE UNBYRONIC HERO:
# EDWARD WAVERLEY AND DON JUAN

'I want a hero. . .'
—Byron, *Don Juan*

Keats declared in 1818 that 'We have seen three literary kings in our Time—Scott—Byron—and then the scotch nove(ls).'[1] Given a few more years' perspective, he could well have altered his statement to discriminate two Byrons as well as two Scotts, for with the commencement of *Don Juan* in 1818, Byron like Scott with his novels made a new departure. One salient difference between *Don Juan* and Byron's other works was the eponymous Don Juan himself.

Byron knew the Don Juan of legend,

> . . . our ancient friend Don Juan—
> We all have seen him, in the pantomine,
> Sent to the devil somewhat ere his time.
> (I.1)

But his own Don Juan is named ironically: he is neither the aggressive seducer nor the demonic figure of tradition. Nor does he fit, as the traditional figure might have, the tradition of the Byronic Hero, since he is lacking in inwardness and passion. Accordingly, we read in a full study of the Byronic Hero that an

> important reason for excluding Don Juan from the family of Byronic Heroes is that he does not seem to share a common paternity: he is, if any-thing, far more closely related to Tom Jones or to Candide than to any of the Romantic heroes.[2]

The reference to an eighteenth-century novel and *conte* is suggestive and has been followed up by a study of *Don Juan and the Eighteenth Century Novel*, which outlines in general terms influential features of the work of three British masters, Fielding, Sterne, and Smollett.[3] However, there is even greater reason for suggesting the influential nature of Scott's novels. As highly successful contemporary works, they suggested what was literarily viable; and their author was linked in Byron's mind with those literary predecessors whom we would certainly regard as significant influences on *Don Juan*. Byron wrote of Scott as the 'Scotch Fielding,' and said that he 'has not been approached, since Cervantes, in depicting manners,' apparently seeing Scott's works in the tradition of the realistic comic epic.[4]

He connected Scott with two other obvious influences on *Don Juan* in this tribute from the work:

> And, as my friend Scott says, 'I sound my warison;'
> Scott, the superlative of my comparative—
> Scott, who can paint your Christian knight or Saracen,
> Serf—Lord—Man, with such skill as none would share it, if
> There had not been one Shakespeare and Voltaire,
> Of one or both of whom he seems the heir.
>                                    (XV.59)

Here Byron stresses the skill and variety of Scott's characterization (with reference to *Last Minstrel* and the medieval novels). Joseph puts well the general influence of Scott's novels when he says that *Don Juan* is

> a historical fantasia, no doubt influenced by the Waverley novels. . . . In Scott he found a model of picaresque narrative, in which the hero is drawn into a series of adventures which involve lively fictitious characters as well as actual historical events; and in the most admired of those, the Scottish novels, the events are not too far removed from the narrator's own time, and the settings are familiar to him. (*Byron the Poet*, p. 179)

Furthermore, some critics have seen in Byron's handling of his materials in *Don Juan* a movement toward a novel-like narrative, and even toward the narrative arrangement of the Waverley novels in particular.[5] My argument is that *Don Juan* owes much to the picaresque novel and the *bildungsroman,* as these are reflected in the Waverley novels. Not only does the hero of *Don Juan* and of Waverley go through a similar pattern of development, but Scott's Waverley Hero is depicted by Scott as morally and historically superseding Byronic Hero-types. In the Waverley novels, then, Byron would have found both a reason for and a method of moving away from his Byronic Hero.

Some simplifying abstraction is involved in speaking of 'the Waverley Hero.' The phrase refers to those main characters who, like Edward Waverley of *Waverley*, are decent but callow young gentlemen who grow to maturity through their participation in historical crisis. A list of them would include Harry Bartram of *The Antiquary*, Lovel of *Guy Mannering*, Henry Morton of *Old Mortality*, Frank Osbaldistone of *Rob Roy*, in the Scottish novels (and Ivanhoe in *Ivanhoe*), but not Jeannie Deans of *The Heart of Mid-Lothian*, or Edgar Ravenswood of *The Bride of Lammer-moor*, or Dugald Dalgetty of *A Legend of Montrose*. There are sufficient similarities amongst the former group to constitute a type: Scott himself referred to them as 'all brethren of a family.'[6]

Much controversy, in part inspired by Scott's review of his own heroes, has surrounded the Waverley Hero to the present day: is he a passive cipher, a mere rhetorical device, or is he a genuine hero in the normative sense, a model of essential humanity? These issues need attention, for there is no record of the way Byron regarded the Waverley Hero. In giving a reading of this hero, I choose the eponymous Edward Waverley for focus, because he is the prototype and would have influenced the reader of subsequent Waverley novels.

## Edward Waverley

*Waverley* is the *bildungsroman* of a young Englishman and the portrait of an age. Edward Waverley begins as a dreamily romantic youth, passes through the bewildering complexities of war, and emerges with a mature moral perspective. His character formation in a perilous world is what commands our attention in the following presentation.

Edward's family background presents in small the two factions which are to collide in war. His father is a Whig opportunist in the Hanoverian government. But since his mother is dead and his father self-absorbed, Edward's upbringing is left to his Jacobite uncle and aunt. This politically divided background contributes to Edward's later divided allegiance between King George and the Jacobite Pretender, Prince Charles Edward. It also helps explain the dreamy, indecisive nature of his character.

The young Edward is of great and unfulfilled potential: he has 'powers of apprehension . . . so quick, as almost to resemble intuition,' and 'a memory of uncommon tenacity' (Ch. iii, pp. 33, 35). These characteristics, coupled with a lack of high animal spirits, make him a reader. But because of a random process of education, Edward learns no self-discipline and becomes a dilettante student.

> The truth was, that the vague and unsatisfactory course of reading which he had pursued, working upon a temper naturally retired and abstracted, had given him that *wavering* and unsettled habit of mind which is most averse to steady and rivetted attention. (Ch. vii, p. 57. My emphasis.)

...₀₀ a dreamer about medieval times, his mind stocked with 'the splendid yet useless imagery and emblems' of chivalric adventure and romantic love (Ch. iv, p. 40). To whatever he was to encounter, Edward's intellect was sure to communicate 'a tincturing of its own romantic tone and colouring' (Ch. v, p. 41).

Like any *bildungsroman* hero—and here we could include Tom Jones, Candide, and, indeed, Byron's Juan—the callow youth must go to the school of experience, here by way of travel and involvement in the turmoil of the Jacobite rebellion of 1745 in Scotland. As in all these works, the young hero's awakening interest in the opposite sex precipitates his setting out into the world. His guardians hurry Edward off with a commission in the English army.

Edward travels to Scotland and, waiting for his troop to arrive, takes a sight-seeing trip to the headquarters of a Scottish bandit chieftain. The exoticism of the Chieftain, Fergus Mac-Ivor, and of his Highlanders is the chief source of color in *Waverley*, but it also symbolizes the romanticism, specifically a Byronic romanticism, which the Waverley Hero must outgrow.

Edward's overactive imagination invests Fergus's campfire with a diabolical aura:

> As he saw it, the red glaring orb seemed to rest on the very surface of the lake itself, and re-sembled the fiery vehicle in which the Evil Genius of an Oriental tale traverses land and sea. (Ch. xvii, p. 119)

Fergus himself is a type from a Byronic Oriental Tale:

> The eyebrow and upper lip bespoke something of the habit of peremptory command and decisive superiority. Even his courtesy, though open, frank, and unconstrained, seemed to indicate a sense of personal importance; and, upon any check or accidental excitation, a sudden, though transient, lour of the eye, showed a hasty, haughty, and vindictive temper, not less to be dreaded because it seemed much under its owner's command. In short, the countenance of the Chieftan resembled a smiling summer's day, in which, notwithstanding, we are made sensible by certain, though slight signs, that it may thunder and lighten before the close of evening. (Ch. xviii, pp. 132-33)

One could compare that other outlaw, Conrad, the Corsair:

> In Conrad's form seems little to admire,
> Though his dark eyebrow shades a glance of fire..
>
> Sun-burnt his cheek, his forehead high and pale

The sable curls in wild profusion veil;
And oft perforce his rising lip reveals
The haughtier thought it curbs, but scarce conceals.

Too close inquiry his stern glance would quell. There breathe but few
whose aspect might defy
The full encounter of his searching eye. . . .

There was a laughing Devil in his sneer,
That raised emotions both of rage and fear;
And where his frown of hatred darkly fell,
Hope withering fled—and Mercy sighed farewell!
(*The Corsair*. I.9.195-96, 203-06, 214-16, 223-26)

As the story continues, Edward comes to see that Fergus and his clan are suited only to an unreal world of the imagination, not to the real world of 1745. Scott's procedure—repeated in several of the novels — is to show that such exotics are, in a word, archaic, that their way of life is too passionate and proud for the prudent compromising and temporizing required by modern life. In the case of the Scottish clans, it is their feudal values which are inadequate. Fergus, as a feudal chieftain, exercises absolute power over the life of his clan and treats clan self-interest as ultimate. His resulting inability to cooperate with others through the fine art of political compromise hurts the Pretender's cause (the uniting of Scotland and subsequent domination of all Britain). The Pretender's political arts cannot satisfy all the clans: at one point, Fergus is enraged at not having been singled out for special favors. The failure of the '45 is implicit in the ensuing bickering of such prima donnas as Fergus. What is more deeply at fault is Fergus's lack of self-discipline. Edward, who eventually excels at organizing and disciplining troops, alone has the abilities which the Highlanders need to succeed in battle.

Fergus's feudal values are also shown to be offensive to modern morality. As clan chieftain, he exercises his prerogative to dispose of his sister Flora in marriage as he wishes; Edward, who is attracted to her and to whom she is offered, unselfishly defends her right to choose for herself. Fergus's clan gives no quarter in battle and no succor to enemy wounded; Edward opposes 'general philanthropy' (Ch. xlv, p. 295) to such barbarism. How out of phase with modern life Fergus and the clans are is made glaringly evident during their march south. Edward observes that Scottish townspeople are totally unmoved by the proclamation of James the Third. Many of them flee.

Of such as remained, the ignorant gazed with astonishment, mixed with
horror ai d aversion, at the wild appearance, unknown language, and
singular garb of the Scottish clans. And to the more prudent, their scanty
numbers, apparent deficiency in discipline, and poverty of equipment,
seemed certain tokens of the calamitous termination of their rash
undertaking. (Ch. lvii, p. 352)

However, Edward's discernment of the inadequacy of the 'romantic' Scots
comes only late in the day, after he has become committed to their cause.
As with Henry Morton, historical crisis obscures for Edward the truth of
events and of motives. Participation in it and the making of mistakes bring
him maturity. It is worthwhile examining Scott's presentation of this
process of maturation, for it is paralleled in key respects by Don Juan, as
we shall see.

Scott has begun with a character of a 'wavering and unsettled habit of
mind.' He has meant 'Waverley' to express Edward's 'wavering' nature;
the turning point in Edward's life comes in Fergus's camp where
Edward's mind 'wavers' over a crucial decision necessitated by events
over which he has no control. The Pretender's threat to the Crown has
become evident and has thrown Edward's visit to a Highland camp in a
bad light. An English newspaper sneers at 'the *Wavering Honour* of W-v-
r-1-y H-n-r' (Ch. xxv, p. 177), with reference to Edward's whole family.
The authorities treat his visit to the camp as treason and summarily
condemn him. We find Edward, thus offended and sentenced, 'bestowing
upon the ruling dynasty that blame which was due to chance, or, in part at
least, to his own unreflecting conduct. . .' (Ch. xxxiii, p. 228). And just at
this moment, with his Hanoverian loyalties wavering, Edward is
befriended by the Pretender. So it is that he transfers loyalties to the
Jacobites; but so it is also that his personal responsibility in the matter is
only partial. It is no serious criticism of Edward that he appears passive,
confused, and drifting in some respects: this is only a fair reflection of an
inexperienced young man's response to the disordered times in which he
lives.

When Edward plunges on into preparations for the campaign, which is to
culminate in the battle of Preston Pans (English: Culloden), his character
takes on a more decisive (unwavering) cast (though, one must admit, the
development seems abrupt):

His person promised firmness and agility, to which the ample folds of the
tartan added an air of dignity. His blue eyes seemed of that kind,
'Which melted in love, and which kindled in war;'

and an air of bashfulness, which was in reality the effect of want of habitual intercourse with the world, gave interest to his features, without injuring their grace or intelligence.(Ch. xlii, p. 273)

At the Ball in the court of the Pretender, when the situation calls for 'a manly and a decisive tone of conduct,' Edward responds by exerting 'his powers of fancy, animation, and eloquence' (although we are given no more than such descriptions as evidence—his speech is always stiff and formal), and the Pretender finds him 'fascinating' (Ch. xliii, p. 284). Finally, on the eve of Culloden, Edward repents his past 'indolence and indecision of mind' (Ch. xlv, p. 296). In battle he is a cool discipliner of troops, though the effort is in vain with the Highlanders. He also gives water to a wounded English soldier whom the clansmen would kill, and acts to save the English Colonel Talbot from a Scottish battle-axe:

Waverley intercepted and prevented the blow, and the officer, perceiving further resistance unavailing, and struck with Edward's generous anxiety for his safety, resigned the fragment of his sword. . . . (Ch. xlvii, p. 305)

When the rebellion is put down, Edward resolves never to draw a sword in civil combat again. Because of his aid to the English, he is pardoned.

It is worth noting for the following comparison with the handling of Don Juan,that Scott means to have it both ways for Edward: his immersion in morally dubious situations and his safe emergence from them. For example, Edward fights for the Scots but his most emphatic acts are in aid of the English. A similar moral prejudice in Edward's favor is shown when he appears to kill a man: a mob crowds around him, and one man charges him 'with such determination as made the discharge of his pistol an act of self-defence' (Ch. xxx, p. 212). Scott makes the discharge a mechanical and not a willed act, and Edward is 'thrilled with a natural horror at the incident,' for he is not the type to kill anyone. To press the point, Scott indulges in poetic license: the 'dead' man has merely been stunned and is still alive. It is clear Scott means to have it both ways: a hero humane in fact as well as intention.[7] However this may grate on our modern preference for tragic irony, we must acknowledge that for Scott the Waverley Hero embodies the highest values, honor and humanity.

In the final analysis, Edward has become 'a spirit tamed by adversity . . . entitled to say firmly, though perhaps with a sigh, that- the romance of his life was ended, and that its real history had now commenced' (Ch. lx, p. 375). 'Real history' is the less momentous business of everyday life; the romance of Waverley's life has been the dream-like, vertiginous ordeal of historical crisis through which he has been educated. This respectable gentleman is in fact the kind of man who guided England through the later eighteenth century; as one critic puts it, Scott has been 'adumbrating a *paideia* for modern life.'[8]

Scott's *Waverley* discredits the old hero of extreme passions in favor of a less spectacular hero. As Lukacs well put it,

> The 'hero' of a Scott novel is always a more or less mediocre, average English gentleman. He generally possesses a certain, though never outstanding, degree of practical intelligence, a certain moral fortitude and decency which even rises to a capacity for self-sacrifice, but which never grows into a sweeping human passion, is never the enraptured devotion to a great cause.[9]

But Waverley's way is preferable to the way of Fergus: less 'heroic' in a grandiose sense, it is more humane. Above all, it is suited to historical reality, which shows us that mores must change if man is to adapt to the changing circumstances of life.

The interpretation of Edward Waverley given here is a sympathetic one and agrees with that accepted by persuasive critics of Scott such as Kroeber, Hart, Johnson. In general, this reading finds Waverley to be the value center of the novel and therefore the hero as well as the protagonist. But certainly he is no hero in a traditional sense. The traditional hero has been well described by Robert Alter:

> Heroism involves an assertion of the will . . . heroic achievement can take place either through action or through passion. [In the former case] the great man extends himself to do a deed which is beyond the reach of the little man. . . . In the latter case, the act of heroism is the hero's ability to assume a burden of suffering others could not carry. Neither kind of heroism, however, can exist outside a context of absolute solidarity between the hero and his society. The active hero realizes in his achievements a set of ideals which he holds in common with the other members of his society, and his achievements are generally for the sake of others as well as for his own glory. The suffering hero—the ritual scapegoat—voluntarily becomes a victim because the complete devotion he feels for his fellow men makes him willing to suffer for their sake.[10]

Waverley, it is clear, is not distinguished by assertions of will. He acts and suffers, but neither to any notable extent. Furthermore, because he is a foreigner to the Scotland he visits, and because he becomes alienated from his English allegiances, he has lost 'a context of absolute solidarity' with a society. Alter gives this description of the 'anti-hero' of the picaresque novel, who is similarly uprooted.

It is easy enough to see what happens when the organic connection between the hero and his society is seriously impaired. The active hero-has no one but himself to benefit in performing his actions: he becomes the picaro, master opportunist. The suffering hero, on the other hand, discovers that his suffering is meaningless because he has nobody for whom to suffer. Instead of being a ritual victim, he finds himself merely the victim of fate—a fate that seems arbitrary and indifferent to him. Instead of being a scapegoat, he is merely a scapegrace— both a ne'er-do-well and literally 'one who escapes grace.'

From an unsympathetic point of view, Waverley could be declared an opportunist—the English certainly regard him as such when they see him in Scottish uniform. And he certainly feels himself to be the victim of an arbitrary and indifferent fate. But Waverley is with equal certainty no picaroon, no 'ne'er-do-well,' and as a result he does not escape grace. His placement somewhere between the traditional hero and picaresque anti-hero is a result of the particular genius of the Waverley novels. For these novels call into question the concept of a fixed society, of a single set of ideals, and instead show a competition between societies or nations, or between segments of one society or nation. Scott presents an historicized version of modern existential alienation: Edward is outside firm social contexts (but not outside the cosmos). An uncertain citizen of any nation, he strives to be a citizen of humanity. In appealing to a set of ideals which represents a higher solidarity of mankind, above historical crisis, the Waverley Hero achieves a kind of heroism, what one critic speaking of general theories of heroism calls 'the quality of high and essential humanity—in the etymological sense, "kindness."'[11]

Just as Scott defends this concept of heroism for embodying pacific and humane values, so he attacks that concept of heroism which involves willful, violent action, such as has been traditionally represented by bloody prowess in battle. Scott felt such prowess to be implicit in the medieval chivalric concept of heroism and condemned it absolutely—without historical qualification. In *Ivanhoe* there is the scathing irony of this passage describing a tournament at arms:

> Thus ended the memorable field of Ashby-de-la-Zouche, one of the most gallantly-contested tournaments of that age; for although only four knights, including one who was smothered by the heat of his armour, had died upon the field, yet upwards of thirty were desperately wounded, four or five of whom never recovered. Several more were disabled for life; and those who escaped best carried the marks of the conflict to the grave with them. Hence it is always mentioned in the old records as the Gentle and Joyous Passage of Arms of Ashby. (Ch. xii, p. 138)

The direct case against chivalric heroism is made by Rebecca, who is often argued to be the moral center of *Ivanhoe;*

> Alas! . . . what is it . . . save an offering of sacrifice to a demon of vain glory . . . ?
> What remains . . . of all the travail and pain you have endured, of all the tears which your deeds have caused . . . ?
>
> (Ch. xxix, p. 292)

If Scott felt chivalric heroism to be so irresponsible and destructive in the days of *Ivanhoe,* he demonstrated by the rashness of the '45, by the barbarity of the clans, and by the vainglory of Fergus how self-defeating it was in the days of *Waverley,* only 'Sixty Years Since' (subtitle).

This argument for Waverley's kind of heroism may not have been obvious in Scott's time, however, considering that critics in our own have not always held it. Donald Davie, for example, prefers a neutral stance toward Edward, 'an obscurely likeable young man of no particular distinction, whom we neither judge nor wish to judge.'[12]

Another critic sees Edward as wholly 'passive' and goes on to assail him for his retrograde tendencies.[13] Views such as these find their prototype in Scott's own self-critical review of 1817, which as previously noted was an unsigned review of his own anonymously written novels. As Edgar Johnson explains and cautions, 'In his odd freedom from literary vanity, it amused him to depreciate the talents of the unknown Author. . . . It is hardly an exaggeration to say that half the uncritical cliches of Scott criticism arc drawn from his own self-disparagement.'[14]   Despite its inherent irony, the review is worth examining, for it reveals features of the Waverley Hero which may have entered into Byron's thinking about him and into his creation of Don Juan.

After complaining in the review of the looseness of the narrative organization, Scott moves to 'another leading fault in these novels,' the weakness of the hero:

> . . . the total want of interest which the reader attaches to the character of the hero. Waverley, Brown, or Bertram in *Guy Mannering,* and Level in the *Antiquary,* are all brethren of a family; very amiable and very insipid sort of young men. . . . His chief characters are never actors, but always acted upon by the spur of circumstances, and have their fates uniformly determined by the agency of the subordinate persons.[15]

Scott goes on to give two reasons, wholly rhetorical in scope, for using such a 'hero.' First, the author has usually represented them as foreigners to whom everything in Scotland is strange,—a circumstance which serves as his apology for entering into many minute details which are reflectively, as it were, addressed to the reader through the medium of the hero. While he is going into explanations and details which, addressed directly to the reader, might appear tiresome and unnecessary, he gives interest to them by exhibiting the effect which they produce upon the principal person of his drama, and at the same time obtains a patient hearing for what might otherwise be passed over without attention. (p. 240)

That is, these heroes are observers, serving as conduits for the colorful lore presented by the author. Second,

The insipidity of this author's heroes may be also in part referred to the readiness with which he twists and turns his story to produce some immediate and perhaps temporary effect. This could hardly be done without representing the principal character either as inconsistent or flexible in his principles. The ease with which Waverley adopts, and afterwards forsakes the Jacobite party in 1745, is a good example of what we mean. Had he been painted as a steady character, his conduct would have been improbable. The author was aware of this; and yet, unwilling to relinquish an opportunity of introducing the interior of the Chevalier's military court, the circumstances of the battle of Preston-pans, and so forth, he hesitates not to sacrifice poor Waverley, and to represent him as a reed blown about at the pleasure of every breeze: a less careless writer would probably have taken some pains to gain the end proposed in a more artful and ingenious manner. But our author was hasty, and has paid the penalty of his haste. (pp. 240-41)

This argument disregards the development of the Waverley Hero from dreamy uncertainty to a mature, realism of perspective. Instead, it sees him as wholly pliable, allowing for complete narrative flexibility.

We may term Scott's review account of the Waverley Hero rhetorical rather than normative in emphasis. There is a half-truth in the review's approach. The details of historical process are best illustrated by a hero who is a good observer, whose very averageness does not allow him to pre-empt the scene he observes. As Lukacs has explained, the hero of an historical fiction which has as part of its purpose the portrait of an age is best presented as a

'middle-of-the-road' hero. Those very social and human characteristics which banish such figures from drama or permit them only a subordinate, episodic role, qualify them for their central position in the historical novel. The relative lack of contour to their personalities, the absence of passions which would cause them to take up major, decisive, one-sided positions,

their contact with each of the contending hostile camps etc. make them
specially suited, to express adequately, in their own destinies, the complex
ramification of events in a novel.[16]

But we have seen that this rhetorical function has its normative
implications: Edward is an Everyman, a morally significant medium for
the presentation of man's historical condition. Bearing in mind both his
normative function as humane hero, and his rhetorical function as symbolic observer, we are in a good position to analyze Byron's Don Juan,
who raises the same issue of the proportion of rhetorical to normative
function.

## Don Juan

Rhetorically, Juan's function is quite similar to that Scott ascribed to
the Waverley Hero. After being sent off from home, he is a foreigner 'to
whom everything . . . is strange,' allowing the author to go 'into explanations and details,' though to be sure the narrator of *Don Juan* goes far
beyond the mere providing of information or even ironic commentary.
Indeed, so much complex awareness is possessed by the narrator that Juan
has relatively little consciousness that we can see. It has been argued that
Juan lives 'in the world while somehow remaining unaffected by it,'[17] and
he may be seen, indeed, as a device serving the author's purposes of
exposition.

Scott's second description of the rhetorical advantage of the Waverley
Hero concerned his pliability, his being 'inconsistent or flexible in his
principles,' thus giving the author freedom in directing his plot. Juan's
many amorous involvements argue his flexibility of principle. His
participation in the treacherous Russian Siege of Ismail seems inconsistent
with his pretention to humaneness—one could compare Scott's statement
about 'the ease with which Waverley adopts . . . the Jacobite part.' When
we last see Juan, he is enjoying the hospitality of the wealthy in England,
another possible inconsistency with high principle. Indeed, as Byron says
of Juan, 'he had . . . the art of living in all climes with ease' (XV.11), and
one could conclude that he is 'a reed blown about at the pleasure of every
breeze.' When J. G. Lockhart advised in print that Byron 'bring the Don
forthwith to England,' it would seem it was easy enough for Byron to
comply.[18]

Juan's apparent pliability keeps most critics from the attempt to see
any significant pattern to his activities: 'his actions do not form a
meaningful sequence leading him towards definitive achievement'; he is
'perilously near being a mere unrelated succession of states of mind'; he

'fails to grow into a substantial and stable consciousness of himself and his world.'[19] But just as Scott's ironic review did not tell the whole story of the Waverley Hero, so a purely rhetorical account of Juan, as the tool of other characters rid circumstances, is not adequate to a full account of him. He may be treated as the hero of a *bildungsroman* on the pattern of *Waverley*, with a career showing the emergence of significant normative characteristics. Study of that career will allow us to see that Byron's concept of heroism has become qualified in the direction of Scott's.

The young Juan's early education, like Waverley's, does not fit him for the world of experience: he becomes a dreamily romantic youth, pursuing 'self-communion with his own high soul' (I.91). Like Waverley, Juan can become infatuated with the opposite sex: 'He thought of wood-nymphs and immortal bowers, / And how the goddesses came down to men' (I.94). When his desires extend to a real woman, and he has his initial scrape with reality by fighting her husband, his mother packs him off into the wide world for safety. But of course there he experiences reality even more thoroughly. In *Don Juan* as Byron left it, Juan moves through two sets of similar events, each set including amorous involvements and a cataclysm; one set occupies the first six cantos, the other the remaining ones. In each set, Juan suffers his outrageous fortunes as part of a pattern of maturation in which he reveals more integrity than he has been given credit for.

In the amorous episodes of the first six cantos, Juan is not merely passive, 'seduced rather than a seducer,' conventional criticism notwithstanding. His involvement with Donna Julia is against both their conscious designs; it is explained naturalistically as being a result of the climate, their ages, their proximity, their naive belief in Platonic love (I.115-16). Juan enters the relation with Haidee freely: 'Happiness was born a twin' (II. 172). In the Turkish harem, Juan is marked for a liaison he dislikes, and so he resists Gulbayez: 'The prisoned eagle will not pair, nor I / Serve a Sultana's sensual phantasy' (V.126). The night with Dudu in the harem results from a sympathy and proximity unexpected by either. In no case is Juan 'seduced' (made the victim of another's will).

The ending of each involvement also reveals Juan's forthrightness in maintaining his own integrity. Confronted by Julia's husband, 'Juan throttled him to get away' (I.186); he manfully resists Lambro's request for his sword, 'Not while this arm is free' (IV.40), provoking a fight; and he prudently escapes the pleasing but dangerous dalliance with Gulbayez.

Juan's integrity, in this early part of *Don Juan*, is highlighted by his performance in the cataclysmic storm (Canto II), where he is invested with nothing less than a stoic heroism. When shipwreck is imminent, Juan exhorts the sailors who hope to die drunk, 'No! / 'Tis true that Death awaits both you and me, / But let us die like men, not sink below / Like brutes' (II.36). It has been observed that the word 'brutes' is one of many Dantean allusions in this whole episode, and is the language used by Dante's Ulysses in his noble speech to his own sailors.[20]

Warring with the attempt by Juan to maintain a high standard of humanity are the forces of Nature, which are obliquely presented as malevolent, through a simile comparing the darkness of night to a veil over 'one whose hate is masked but to assail' (II.49). When the urgings of 'Nature' (II.75) drive many of the sailors to cannibalism, Juan is one of the few to refuse to eat either his spaniel or the luckless Pedrillo. If Juan cannot resist 'Nature' in his affair with Julia—a matter of lesser seriousness—he can resist it where it would seriously diminish his humanity.

The storm and the loss of idyllic love with Haidee are not merely colorful episodes allowing the narrator to indulge in virtuoso digressions: they also constitute felt experiences for Juan. On arriving in Turkey, he can tell his new comrade Johnson that 'I have borne / Hardships which have the hardiest overworn, / On the rough deep' (V.18-19). He has begun to change, though it be only slightly: 'Juan was juvenile, and thus was full, / As most at his age are, of hope, and health; / Yet I must own, he looked a little dull. . .' (V.8), for, the narrator continues, he had suffered 'things to shake a Stoic; ne'ertheless, / Upon the whole his carriage was serene' and 'some gilded remanants' remain in his dress (V.9). When Johnson counsels resignation with the reflection that 'Time strips our illusions of their hue' (V.21), Juan coolly answers that 'All this is very fine, and may be true, / . . . but I really don't see how / It betters present times with me or you' (V.23). Juan once again, as in the open-boat exercise, shows a stoical fortitude which he will now allow events or Johnson's philosophizing to compromise.

Juan has, then, a portion of that endurance shown by the Doge Foscari—a hero Byron developed within a year after writing Canto V. When he wrote the next cantos, however—perhaps as a result of already having explored the hero of suppressed passion—Byron put Juan through a course of experience which at least raises questions about Juan's character. I shall argue that these questions are no more finally damaging to Juan than was Edward's participation in the rash adventure of the '45.

At issue are the Russian cantos, VII-X, in which Juan participates in the 1790 Siege of Ismail, a Turkish fortress, and lives for a while in the Russian court. The pattern reminds one of Waverley's joining the Jacobite forces and entering the Pretender's court.

The Siege is a man-made version of the sea-ordeal of Canto II: 'Let there be Blood! says man, and there's a sea!' (Vii.41). Whereas Byron only implied malevolent purpose in nature's cataclysm, he explicitly identifies it in man's: the Siege represents not a cause which is 'one to which a good heart could be partial— / Defense of freedom, country, or of laws,' but instead one which reveals 'mere lust of Power to o'er-arch all / With its proud brow' (VII.40), that oppression of liberty which Byron consistently deplored throughout his life.[21] The ruthless commander of the Siege, Russian Marshal Suvarov (in Byron's usage, Souvaroff and Suwarrow), 'Who calculated life as so much dross, / And as the wind a widowed nation's wail' (VI.lxxvii), is representative of those 'heroes' defined by their bloody military prowess. One must deal with the fact that Juan fights for his evil cause.

It is not plausible, however, to go so far in faulting Juan for participating in the battle as some critics have done: one finds that Byron 'lances him with irony for his part in the battle'; another, that 'The Criticism of Juan deepens when the narrator reminds us that greathearted and gently loving though Juan may be, he, without the slightest awareness that he does so, leaves a trail of bodies behind him. . . . The attacks on Juan are just heavy enough to call into question his way of life. . . .'[22] One could speculate that Juan has just had his sex and his integrity threatened in a Turkish harem and now embraces the chance to fight Turks. In any case, he and Johnson confront the imposing figure of Suvarov himself, who pays Juan the compliment of making him the leader of the assault. Waverley, when similarly adrift after feeling betrayed by England, was happy to accept the identity conferred upon him by Fergus and later by Prince Charles. But neither Edward nor Juan embraces his new cause with deep ideological commitment or sense of guilt—Juan is no Alp. Rather, each with justification takes sides in a crisis when he feels himself intolerably threatened by one faction and protected by the other.

Edward and Juan, finding themselves in battle, are both infected with its excitement. As the Highlanders advance at Culloden,

> Waverley felt his heart at that moment throb as it would have burst from his bosom. It was not fear, it was not ardour,—it was a compound of both, a new and deeply energetic impulse, that with its first emotion chilled and astounded, then fevered and maddened his mind. The sounds around him combined to exalt his enthusiasm; the pipes played, the clans rushed forward . . . the muttering sounds of the men to each other began to swell into a wild cry. (Ch. xlvii, p, 304)

Byron, too, however much he disapproves of it, presents the attack as impressive:

A mirrored Hell! the volleying roar, and loud   Long booming of each peal
on peal, o'ercame
The ear far more than thunder. . . .
(VIII.6)

Juan, like Edward, is fevered and maddened with the excitement:

But *here* he was!—where each tie that can bind
Humanity must yield to steel and flame:
And *he* whose very body was all mind,
Flung here by Fate or Circumstance, which tame
The loftiest, hurried by the time and place,
Dashed on like a spurred blood-horse in a race.
So was his blood stirred while he found resistance. . . .
(VIII.54-55)

Byron's focus is the 'Fate or Circumstance' which has thrown Juan into
this cataclysm, rather than any depths of evil in Juan. Several features of
his description of Juan serve to lessen any criticism of Juan himself.

First, no description of Juan is given which does not immediately
widen to include the behavior of mankind in general: 'if he must needs
destroy . . . [he does so] In such good company as always throng / To
battles, sieges, and that kind of pleasure' (VIII.24); 'The thirst / Of Glory,
which so pierces through and through one, / Pervaded him . . .' (VIII.52).
Second, Byron qualifies Juan's violent acts with mitigating descriptions of
his true character: if he destroys, it is 'always without malice' (VIII.25); if
he is pervaded by a thirst for glory, it is in spite of his being 'a generous
creature, / As warm in heart as feminine in feature' (VIII.52). When Juan
participates in the killing of the Tartar Khan, a figure Byron clearly
admires, it is only after he and Johnson have begged him 'for God's sake,
just to show / So much less fight as might form an apology / For *them* in
saving such a desperate foe' (VIII.108). Juan falls to the killing 'with
sighs' (VIII.109), as if regretful. These mitigating statements and the
deflection of attention away from Juan alone are Byron's way of
withholding his hero from true depravity; Scott does the same by
exempting his heroes from killing in battle.

Finally, Byron enhances Juan's stature in the same way Scott did
Waverley's, by having him perform an act of 'general philanthropy' in the
heat of battle—'one good action in the midst of crimes' (VIII.40). Just as
Waverley had stopped his comrades from killing Colonel Talbot, so Juan
fights, wounding two of his comrades, 'villanous Cossacques' (VIII.92), to
keep them from slaughtering a little girl, Leila: 'Whatsoever is to be /
Done, I'll not quit her till she seems secure / Of present life a good deal

more than we' (VIII.100). The more pragmatic Johnson would have Juan abandon her: 'we've no time to lose . . . now choose / Between your fame and feelings, pride and pity' (VIII.101). Juan apparently chooses the latter qualities, for he is 'immovable' (VIII.102). After the battle, Juan is decorated for behaving 'with courage and humanity' (VIII.140).

Juan's next adventure raises questions about his moral sensitivity just as the battle did. He enters the gay life of Catherine's court, 'a hurry / Of waste, and haste, and glare, and gloss, and glitter' (X.26) much as Waverley enters 'the liveliness and elegance' (Ch. xliii, p. 280) of the Ball at Charles's court. Juan falls into 'self-love' (IX.68) from Catherine's flattery of him; Waverley, before the Ball, 'looked at himself in the mirror more than once, and could not help acknowledging that the reflection seemed that of a very handsome young fellow' (Ch. xlii, p. 273). Thus both young heroes seem blinded by the glamour of high places. Again, as in Juan's joining the Siege, Byron gives us cause to suspect his integrity. Whereas before he had resisted the imperious Gulbayez, now with Catherine he enters one of those 'Unequal matches, such as are, alas! / A young Lieutenant's with a *not old* queen. . . ' (X.24); in short, 'Don Juan grew, I fear, a little dissipated' (X.23). But again, Juan has not sunk into serious depravity, as the generalized and qualified descriptions attest. Also, there is the mitigating circumstance that Juan grows sick while with Catherine (X.39—from unspecified causes), and continues his loving attentions to Leila. More than a reflection on Juan's depravity, the Russian Cantos are a testimony to the imperial lust which expresses itself in battlefield and bedroom.

That the Russian court corruption did not agree with Juan's true character is seen by his behavior on arrival in England, where he recovers some of his former idealism and spirit. He wishes to see England as 'Freedom's chosen station . . . [where] none lay / Traps for the traveller' (XI.9-10). When just after this statement a highwayman waylays him, Juan does not become depressed but fights back unhesitatingly. It is clear that once again Byron will show how the ways of the world clash with Juan's idealism, but this is not to say, as one critic has, that Juan's resilience means he is a perpetually grinning 'booby.'[23]

In fact, he is now further shadowed by experience than he was on arrival at the Turkish harem. Lady Pinchbeck sees him as 'a good heart at bottom, / A little spoiled, but not so altogether,' and the narrator thinks this a wonder, considering

. . . how he had been tossed, he scarce knew whither:
Though this might ruin others, it did *not* him At least entirely—for he had

seen too many Changes in Youth, to be surprised at any.
                                                    (XII.44)

In matters of love, Juan is likewise tarnished,

A little blasé—'tis not to be wondered
At, that his heart had got a tougher rind:
And though not vainer from his past success,
No doubt his sensibilities were less.
                                    (XII.81)

Juan's past has constituted, then, a process of maturation for him, although, as with Edward, we have not been taken extensively inside his thought processes by the author. Just as we found that Edward emerges rather suddenly with 'a manly and a decisive tone of conduct,' so we read that Juan's 'conduct, since in England, grew more / Strict, and his mind assumed a manlier vigour' (XV.11); and where Edward to our surprise is exerting 'his powers of fancy, animation, and eloquence' (Ch. xliii, p. 283), Juan displays 'talent and good humour' and 'marked distinction' (XII.85). Scott issued a pretty portrait of Edward—'He' s a pretty man—a very pretty man,' says Evan Dhu—as possessing 'firmness and agility . . . an air of dignity . . . blue eyes . . . which melted in love, and which kindled in war; . . . grace and intelligence . . .' (Ch. xlii, p. 273). And so Byron's final disposition of Juan finds him with the same social presence: well-behaved, self-possessed, circumspect, experienced, and capable:

                        14
By nature soft, his whole address held off
Suspicion: though not timid, his regard
Was such as rather seem'd to keep aloof,
To shield himself than put *you* on your guard:
Perhaps 't was hardly quite assured enough,
But Modesty's at times its own reward,
Like Virtue; and the absence of pretension
Will go much farther than there's need to
Mention.

                        15
Serene, accomplish'd, cheerful but not loud;
Insinuating without insinuation;
Observant of the foibles of the crowd,
Yet ne'er betraying this in conversation;
Proud with the proud, yet courteously proud,
So as to make them feel he knew his station

And theirs:—without a struggle for priority,
He neither brooked nor claimed superiority.
                                        (Canto XV)

That Juan did not claim superiority is final evidence that his involvement with the lusts of Prussian imperialism did not subvert his basic decency. He is, finally, a figure of that stature attainable by a decent young man who is 'a little superficial' (XI.51), but is above the commonalty, a 'Gentleman!' as we are frequently reminded (q.v. V.9; IX.83; XI.84; XII.30). Juan is thus, like Edward, fitted to make his mark in the affairs of man—'able / For Love, War, or Ambition' (X.22). 'Our Hero—as a hero—young and handsome, / Noble, rich, celebrated . . .' (XI.74) is like Jane Austen's Emma, 'handsome . . . and rich,' but like Edward differs from her in not being so 'clever' as to become lost in the labyrinths of excessive self-involvement. That quality is reserved for Byronic Heroes and Fergus Mac-Ivors.

The point of the foregoing demonstration has been to show that Don Juan is not the cipher or booby that critics have sometimes held him to be, but may be understood in terms of the Waverley Hero who, I have argued, touches one meaning of the heroic. This conclusion is not so surprising when we realize that in *Don Juan* Byron attempted a version of the feat Scott had accomplished in his novels, the creation of an historical panorama of recent modern times. (*Waverley* is subtitled 'Tis Sixty Years Since'; *Don Juan* begins roughly thirty years since.) Juan is rhetorically the proper hero for such a venture. Normatively, he is similar to Edward in avoiding the excesses of the Byronic Hero. While both young heroes can become lost owing to the confusions of youth and the pressure of circumstance, both maintain a high degree of personal integrity and basic humaneness.

Withal, there is a different emphasis in the two authors' treatments of the overall careers of their heroes. For the Waverley Hero, experience educates, from a dreamy vagueness to a realistic perspective. This pattern of growth is a reflection of Scott's rationalism, in which 'romantic' is synonymous with dreams and fancies. Byron is more truly Romantic in the Wordsworthian sense. For the Romantic, the course of experience involves spiritual loss: man falls when he is born and falls deeper as he lives. Juan begins as a dreamy youth, but those dreams include admirable ideals which experience erodes. Thus Juan's 'sensibilities are less' in the matter of love, and, Byron implies by the contrast provided by the initially hopeful Haidee affair, it is a sad thing. Scott makes a similar point, but only tentatively, when he describes Edward as 'entitled to say firmly . . . though perhaps with a sigh, that the romance of his life was ended, and that its real history had now commenced.' The 'sigh' is Scott's concession to what is lost, concomitant with his conviction that the conditions of modern life must be embraced. It is on this matter that he and Byron differ. Scott could on the whole endorse the point to which history had developed: he supported the Tory establishment and the Peace of Versailles. Byron, on the contrary, saw Versailles as the re-establishment of 'the unity / Of Tyrants' (IX.9), and, indeed, formally dedicated *Don Juan* to an attack on the establishment forces in Britain, as represented by Southey and Castlereagh, both of them good friends of Scott. He could well doubt that Juan's experience would lead to an increase in wisdom or even to survival, though the matter remained open to the uncertainties of the future.

It is appropriate to conclude this examination of the unByronic Hero of *Don Juan* by observing that Byron had developed a definite concept of heroism but was uncertain that the modern world would afford many opportunities for the expression of that heroism. His concept may be defined: stoic endurance as regards one's self; service to humanity as regards the objective world. Some critics seem so preoccupied with Byron's disappointment over Napoleon that they would deny Byron's endorsement of heroism or of heroism in the modern world.[24] In fact, Napoleon for Byron was but a recent failure, the anti-type of the modern hero, Washington. For himself, Washington 'scorned great recompenses'; for humanity, he enjoyed the 'all-cloudless glory (which few men's is) / To free his country' (IX.8). To Byron's mind, then, such heroic greatness was rare but not nonexistent.

Byron's works present many varieties of the incomplete realization of this full heroism. The Byronic Hero suffers greatly, but in scorning humanity or refusing to attempt to serve it, fails at full heroism. Faliero and Sardanapalus both seem finally deficient in the capacity for endurance. The Doge Foscari is the one hero who greatly combines endurance and service to humanity, but at tragic cost to his own humanity. Don Juan possesses both attributes at a modest level but is not yet put forth as an effective leader: he survives, but it is not clear whether his good qualities, like those of the Waverley Hero, will prevail. To assert that they might must, to Byron, have been a matter requiring existential ratification. In his last complete work, *The Island,* Byron entertained the fancy, not that his modest hero would be triumphant in history, but that he deserved to escape its terrors. *The Island* is Byron's most Scottian work, for it is an exercise in hopefulness.

# Notes

[1] *The Letters of John Keats: 1814-21*, ed. Hyder Edward Rollins, 2 vols. (Cambridge, Mass.: Harvard Univ. Press, 1958), II, 16 (to the George Keatses, ca. 29 Dec.).

[2] Peter Thorslev, *The Byronic Hero; Types and Prototypes* (Minneapolis: Univ. of Minnesota Press, 1962), p. 13.

[3] Andras Horn (Bern: A. Francke, 1962).

[4] *BLJ.* 8, 13 (Diary. 5 Jan. 1821); to Pryse Gordon Lockhart, 3-6 May 1816, in Lovell, *His Very Self*, p. 180.

[5] John Speirs, *Poetry Towards Novel* (London: Faber, 1971), pp. 216-82; Kroeber, *Romantic Narrative Art*, pp. 136-37.

[6] Unsigned review of 'Tales of My Landlord, 1817,' in *Quarterly Review.* XVI (1817), rpt. Ioan Williams, ed. *Sir Walter Scott on Novelists and Fiction* (London: Routledge, 1968), p. 240.

[7] Scott violates probability to make sure his heroes have 'clean hands.' Both Halbert Glendinning (*The Monastery*) and Roland Graeme (*The Abbot*) 'kill' someone, but the killing turns out to have been only apparent.

[8] Avrom Fleishman, *The Historical Novel: Walter Scott to Virginia Woolf* (Baltimore: Johns Hopkins Press, 1971), p. 52.

[9] *Historical* Novel, p. 33.

[10] This and the following quotation are from *Rogue's Progress: Studies in the Picaresque Novel* (Cambridge, Mass.: Harvard Univ. Press, 1964), pp. 72-73.

[11] Brian Wilkie, *Romantic Poets and Epic Tradition* (Madison: Univ. of Wisconsin Press, 1965), p. 20.

[12] *The Heyday of Sir Walter Scott* (London: Routledge, 1961), p. 25.

[13] Alexander Welsh, *The Hero of the Waverley Novels* (New Haven: Yale Univ. Press, 1963).

[14] *Scott,* pp. 522-23.

[15] *On Novelists*, p. 240, subsequent page citations in context.

[16] *Historical Novel*, p. 128.

[17] Wilkie, *Romantic* Poets, p. 213.

[18] *John Bull's Letter to Lord Byron*, ed. Alan Lang Strout (1821; rpt. Norman, Okla.: Univ. of Oklahoma Press, 1947), p. 98.

[19] Wilkie, *Romantic Poets*, p. 212; Lovell, *Byron*, p.224; Cooke, *The Blind Man*, pp. 195-96.

[20] Wilkie, *Romantic Poets.* p. 204, citing *Inferno.*XXVI, 118-20.

[21] See Wilfred S. Dowden, 'The Consistency of Byron's Social Doctrine,' Rice Institute Pamphlets, XXXVII, No. 3 (Oct. 1950), 18-44.

[22] Cooke, *The Blind Man*, p. 196; Alvin B. Kernan, *The Plot of Satire* (New Haven: Yale Univ. Press, 1965), pp. 201-02.

[23] Kernan, *Plot of Satire*, p. 201.

[24] E.g., Cooke, who coins the phrase 'counter-heroism' to express Byron's concept of essential humanity as a combination of humanism and stoicism (*The Blind Man*,

pp. 181-82); and Wilkie, who holds that Byron saw pacific and spiritual values as being at odds with 'heroism' (*Romantic Poets*, p. 225).

# CHAPTER FIVE

## CULTURAL CONFRONTATION: ROMANCE AND REALITY

From childhood's earliest hour my heart rebelled against the
influence of external circumstances in myself and others.
—Scott, *Journal*

In the midst of writing the English Cantos of *Don* Juan, Byron turned
aside to write *The Island* (in January-February 1823), after the completion
of Canto XIV). Whereas in the whole of *Don Juan* Byron realistically por-
trays the structures and forces—family, war, royal courts, moneyed
society—which hedge the individual's freedom, in *The Island* he allows
himself a letting off of pressure, an indulgence in a romance vision of
escape from the dragons of modern history. Byron indeed creates what
one critic calls 'a new paradise safe from the world's slow stain,' but it is a
highly qualified 'paradise,' because Byron is aware that South Sea Island
life is a part of this world and has its place in history.[1] He de-emphasizes
these realistic qualifications, but makes it clear that Island life is
paradisaical only relative to modern European life, and then only when we
ignore the terrors of nature and tribal life.

In pitting Island life against modern civilization, Byron comes close to
Scott's characteristic presentation of cultural confrontations between
traditional and progressive life styles. For Scott, the confrontation is
dialectical, making for evolution. The archaic life style is the older one on
the continuum of history, and it yields to the modern, newer. In Byron's
*The Island,* there is only polarity, not dialectic, a highlighting of alter-
native life styles. The modern is old, as a human being grows old; the
archaic is new, an infancy, a new beginning within a cyclical concept of
history.[2] But both authors are ambivalent in their handling of the clash or
contrast of life styles, being romantically attracted to the archaic, but
realistically committed to dealing with the modern. A general account of
the dialectic presented in the Waverley novels will provide a useful
background for understanding the powerful contradiction of allegiances
Byron expresses in *The Island.*

# Scott

## (1) Cultural Relativity of Values

David Daiches has explained the springs of Scott's literary imagination:

> Scott's attitude to life was derived from his response to the fate of his own country: it was the complex of feelings with which he contemplated the phase of Scottish history immediately preceding his own time that provided the point of view which gave life—often a predominantly tragic life—to these novels. Underlying most of these novels is a tragic sense of the inevitability of a drab but necessary progress, a sense of the impotence of the traditional kind of heroism, a passionately regretful awareness of the fact that the Good Old Cause was lost forever and the glory of Scotland must give way to her interest.[3]

The Waverley novels for the most part deal with this painful but inevitable and necessary birth of the present out of the dialectic of older with more modern ways. Always the older ways lose, but ethically the opposition is never simple. We have seen that both factions of the dialectic can be represented by inhumane extremists, the Burleys and Claverhouses. Likewise, both sides contain something of value. In *Old Mortality*, for example, the commander-in-chief of the victorious government forces is the wise, capable Duke of Monmouth, a monument to the ideal of the gentleman. The problem is, however, that when the forces of the older ways lose, what they also contain of value may be lost.

The following passage gives us a sense of the nobility often to be found in the older ways. In it, Evan Maccombich, one of Fergus's (gaelic: Vich Ian Vohr) lieutenants, responds to the prospect of a death sentence against his chieftain:

> 'I was only ganging to say, my Lord,' said Evan, in what he meant to be in an insinuating manner, 'that if your excellent honour, and the honourable Court, would let Vich Ian Vohr go free just this once, and let him gae back to France, and no to trouble King George's government again, that ony six o' the very best of his clan will be willing to be justified in his stead; and if you'll just let me gae down to Glenna-quoich, I'll fetch them up to ye mysell, to head or hang, and you may begin wi' me the very first man.
>
> 'Notwithstanding the solemnity of the occasion, a sort of laugh was heard in the court at the extraordinary nature of the proposal. The Judge checked this indecency, and Evan, looking sternly around, when the murmur abated, 'If the Saxon gentlemen are laughing,' he said, 'because a poor man, such as me, thinks my life, or the life of six of my degree, is worth that of Vich Ian Vohr, it's like enough they may be very right; but if

they laugh because they think I would not keep my word, and come back to redeem him, I can tell them they ken neither the heart of a Hielandman, nor the honour of a gentleman.'

There was no further inclination to laugh among the audience, and a dead silence ensued.

The Judge then pronounced upon both prisoners the sentence of the law of high treason, with all its horrible accompaniments. The execution was appointed for the ensuing day. 'For you, Fergus Mac-Ivor,' continued the Judge, 'I can hold out no hope of mercy. You must prepare against to-morrow for your last sufferings here, and your great audit hereafter.'

'I desire nothing else, my lord,' answered Fergus, in the same manly and firm tone.

The hard eyes of Evan, which had been perpetually bent on his Chief, were moistened with a tear. 'For you, poor ignorant man,' continued the Judge, 'who, following the ideas in which you have been educated, have this day given us a striking example how the loyalty due to the king and state alone, is, from your unhappy ideas of clanship, transferred to some ambitious individual, who ends by making you the tool of his crimes — for you, I say, I feel so much compassion, that if you can make up your mind to petition for grace, I will endeavour to procure it for you. Otherwise'—

'Grace me no grace,' said Evan; 'since you are to shed Vich Ian Vohr's blood, the only favour I would accept from you is—to bid them loose my hands and gie me my claymore, and bide you just a minute sitting where you are!' (*Waverley*. Ch. lxviii, pp. 422-23)

Maccombich's plea, based on the great feudal value of the chieftain, is eloquent, noble, and touching but quite absurd in the context of a modern court of law, where all individuals are equal. One life style, with its high code of values, is thus quite out of place within the controlling sphere of another code, providing us with an object lesson in the cultural relativity of values. When these different cultures are juxtaposed, a fearful dialectic ensues whose only resolution is war, with an inevitable but regrettable loss of much of the old nobility.

## (2) Romance and Reality

We have noted that Scott represents the strangeness and wonder of these older ways as *like* a Romance world, but only as seen through the eyes of his dreamy hero. A Fergus seems to be an Oriental tale villain, a Madge Wildfire (*The Heart of Mid-Lothian*) seems to be a witch, but there are rational explanations for such creatures. The Romance element of the Waverley novels does not pertain to these appearances of the supernatural and fanciful: the unreal has no positive existence for Scott. (*The Bride of Lammermoor* is a special case, discussed below.)

The *unrealistic* does. The Stuart and Covenanter causes, for example, despite the good intentions and the passionate sincerity of their adherents, are unrealistic. They lack those drabbest but most necessary modern qualities of organization and discipline, without which no cause can hope to succeed. Scott shows Waverley and Morton trying in vain to discipline the rebel armies. The English armies are by comparison efficient war machines, and they triumph, representatives of 'a drab but necessary progress' discerned by Scott's sense of realism.

The romance aspect of a Waverley novel lies in the rewarding pattern of experience projected for the hero: he encounters the dragons of cultural conflict but is not destroyed in their clash; he carries forward into the modern something of the older values, and his life has a 'comic' resolution symbolized by his harmonious reintegration into society, usually through a marriage which unites previously opposed factions.

Waverley's nightmarish displacement from routine existence into war and his survival of its threat to his entire identity is thus 'the romance of his life,' and he transcends it into 'the real history' of his life. In like manner, Morton is not executed but only exiled for his role in the rebellion; moreover, the Glorious Revolution of 1688 allows his pardon and return from exile and the working out of the unsettled score with his nemesis, Burley, and his love, Edith. Both Waverley and Morton marry women who represent the faction they have opposed, symbolically resolving the cultural conflict.

In all the Waverley novels, with one exception, Scott superimposes upon tragically realistic settings a comic romance pattern of experience, motivated by his serious moral vision—partly optimistic, partly wishful— of a right resolution of historical dialectic. How hopeful and tentative such resolutions are is revealed by an exception which proves the rule, *The Bride of Lammermoor* (1819).

In *The Bride*, Edgar Ravenswood, a true Scott moderate, attempts to transcend an inherited feud between the ancient house of Ravenswood and that of the *parvenu* Ashtons, through the forces of reason and love. His rationalism restrains him from entering this feud, from taking sides in the bitter factional politics of the period, and from believing in the portents and prophecies which provide an atmosphere of Gothic fatality. His love for Lucy Ashton promises a marriage which will bridge the schism between the two families. As Hart puts it, Ravenswood's 'virtues and the values governing the book make it unambiguously desirable [that he should] escape his bloody heritage.'[4] But he does not. The Gothic Romance atmosphere and the realistic developments of character and circumstance combine in a tragic ending: Lucy goes mad over her mother's schemings against Edgar and dies; and Ravenswood dies when he rides into quicksand on his way to a duel with her brother, who has charged him with responsibility for her death. The tragedy is presented as fated and reverses the terms of the other Waverley novels: the representatives of old and new perish together; there is no transcendence of historical fatality.

The story of the composition of *The Bride* reveals the reasons for the work's peculiarities. Lockhart tells us it was composed by dictation front the sick bed, Scott groaning in pain. When handed the finished product, Scott could recollect nothing of it. Edgar Johnson comments: 'Released by Scott's illness, his imagination dredged up primitive terrors from primordial depths . . . things . . . that Scott's waking mind rejected.'[5] *The Bride* represents, then, the triumph of the nightmarish forces of history (acting through the inherited feud) which Scott's typical work shows to be surmounted.

If *The Bride* is Scott's *Christabel* of nightmarish engulfment, *The Island* is Byron's 'Kubla Khan' of daydreamed enchantment. Written in the midst of Don Juan's unresolved involvement with the forces of history, the tale reverses Byron's depiction of the hero defeated by the forces of this world, and shows a hoped-for transcendence. It, too, is an exception proving the rule.

*The Island* contains in fuller measure than *Don Juan* the motifs of the Waverley novel: the contrast of different cultures; the conditioning of the individual by his culture; a Byronic hero who perishes from his own extremism; a sympathetic representative of authority; a Waverley hero, modest and inherently good, a mediator between the two cultures; and the juxtaposition of a comic romance pattern upon a tragically realistic situation. These motifs will become evident in the following detailed discussion of Byron's last long poem.

# Byron

## (1) Cultural Relativity of Values

*The Island* is structured on the contrast of the life style of the inhabitants of the South Sea island 'Toobonai' and the life style of European visitors in thc persons of English sailors. Let us first examine Byron's exposition of Toobonai; then we shall examine the Englishmen who provide the narrative force.

The South Seas setting is conveyed in hushed, warm, loving accents. The ship entering these seas 'gently made her liquid way' (I.1.2) into a world of placid naturalistic fullness and life-enhancement:

> the luxurious silence of the skies, The sweet siesta of a summer day,
> The tropic afternoon of Toobonai,
> When every flower was bloom, and air was balm, And the first breath began to stir the palm,
> The first yet voiceless wind to urge the wave All gently to refresh the thirsty cave. . . .
>      (II.6.104-10)

Man here seems free of Adam's curse of work and Cain's competition with his brother:

> The gentle island, and the genial soil,
> The friendly hearts, the feasts without a toil,
> The courteous manners but from nature caught,
> The wealth unhoarded, and the love unbought. . . .
>                (I.6.107-10)

> Nature, and Nature's goddess—Woman—woos
> To lands where, save their conscience, none accuse;
> Where all partake the earth without dispute,
> And bread itself is gathered as a fruit;
> Where none contest the fields, the woods, the streams:—
> The goldless Age, where Gold disturbs no dreams,
> Inhabits or inhabited the shore.
>                (I.10.211-17)

Circumstance itself seems without force in a land where man has 'no master save his mood' (I.2.38). The living representative of this near-paradise, 'Nature's goddess,' is Neuha, 'In growth a woman, though in years a child' (II.7.124), who serves as man's support, not as the source of his fall:

> Herself a billow in her energies,
> To bear the bark of others' happiness,
> Nor feel a sorrow till their joy grew less.
>                (II.7.142-44)

She represents the fulfillment of love, because she is free from the societal entanglements of an advanced civilization:

Rapt in the fond forgetfulness of life,
Neuha, the South Sea girl, was all a wife,
With no distracting world to call her off
From Love; with no Society to scoff
At the new transient flame; no babbling crowd
Of coxcombry in admiration loud,
Or with adulterous whisper to alloy
Her duty, and her glory, and her joy.
(II.14.332-39)

The young British sailor, Torquil, is her lover, and the two live 'not in earth, but in . . . ecstacy' (II.16.371). They feel themselves to be in an eternal present:

What deemed they of the future or the past?
The present, like a tyrant, held them fast:
Their hour-glass was the sea-sand, and the tide, Like her smooth billow,
saw their moments glide; Their clock the Sun, in his unbounded tower;
They reckoned not, whose day was but an hour.
(II.15.352-57)

Thus a rich accumulation of prelapsarian imagery in all these passages establishes the unique value of Too-bonai life. But just as Scott finds shadows in the colorful life of the Highlands, so Byron finds more in Toobonai than what he called 'the pamby portions.'[6] Toobonai is paradisaical but not paradise, Elysian but not Elysium. The complexity of Byron's account of the island derives from his strong awareness of life as being bound up in historical process.

The first matter to notice is the explicitly European point of view of the narrator. All the descriptions of Toobonai are meaningful only by their contrast with European manners. The wrath the speaker feels for those manners explains the affection he can feel for those of Toobonai, but the values of Toobonai are thereby relative only, not absolute. Two discriminations made by the narrator in his description of the pleasant songs of the island provide illustration:

Thus rose a song—the harmony of times
Before the winds blew Europe o'er these climes.
True, they had vices (such are Nature's growth)
But only the barbarian's—we have both:
The sordor of civilisation, mix'd
With all the savage which Man's fall hath fix'd.
(II.4.65-70)

First we see that Toobonai's virtues are due to lack of contact with European civilization, due really to Toobonai's being in an earlier stage of development. Byron emphasizes throughout the poem that Toobonai is an 'infant world' (II.7.127; IV.14.420—last line of poem), not a world of a different order of reality: it is thus historically located on a continuum leading to modern Europe. The second discrimination is that Toobonai is postlapsarian: if it seems a land of pure goodness, this is only because it has a lesser order of vices. Consequently, the description of Toobonai may be understood as distinctively a European's view, a reaction away from the complexities of the modern world to daydream languishings like those of the young British sailors 'for some sunny isle, / Where summer years and summer women smile' (I.2.27-28).

We can note secondly that both the natural and human worlds of Toobonai have their ominous aspects and history. There will come the time, the narrator sees, when 'the Earthquake [will] tear the Naiad's cave, / Root up the spring, and trample on the wave, / And crush the living waters to a mass, / The amphibious desert of the dark morass!' (II.vii.155-58). The underwater cave to which Torquil and Neuha escape is the result of 'some Earthquake . . . / When the Poles crashed, and water was the world' (IV.7.148-50).

As for the civilization of Toobonai, Carl Woodring has observed that Byron's source, Mariner and Martin's *An Account of the Natives of the Tonga Islands*, shows a people

> under a king and priests in rigid social stratification, strict taboos, murderous suspicion of strangers, frequent child-sacrifices, and well-motivated cannibalism. Apologizing for these few excesses, Mariner and Martin chiefly wanted to show how similar these people were to Europeans. Byron ignored both the cannibalism and the feudal rigor.[7]

Byron avoids most of these dark complexities, but does not completely dehistoricize his account of the island. Neuha is

> Highborn (a birth at which the herald smiles,
> Without a scutcheon for these secret isles),
> Of a long race, the valiant and the free,
> The naked knights of savage chivalry,
> Whose grassy cairns ascend along the shore;
>                               (II.10.214-18)

Not only does Neuha fall within this noble heroic tradition, but there are ancient voices speaking of the ravages of war. In the songs which open

Canto II, a shadow passes across this happy sun-drenched world as the songstress (Neuha) recalls

> The memory bright with many a festival,
> Ere Fiji blew the shell of war, when foes
> For the first time were wafted in canoes.
> Alas! for them the flower of manhood bleeds;
> Alas! for them our fields are rank with weeds:
> Forgotten is the rapture, or unknown,
> Of wandering with the Moon and Love alone.
> But be it so:—*they* taught us how to wield
> The club, and rain our arrows o'er the field:
> Now let them reap the harvest of their art!
> But feast to-night! to-morrow we depart.
> Strike up the dance! the cava bowl fill high!
> Drain every drop—to-morrow we may die.
>                         (II.2.34-46)

Similarly, when Torquil and Neuha go to their underwater cave, with its womb-Cathedral imagery and death-and-rebirth symbolism, Neuha gives an historical account of the previous use of the cave in the midst of warfare:

> How a young Chief, a thousand moons ago,
> Diving for turtle in the depths below,
> Had risen, in tracking fast his ocean prey,
> Into the cave which round and o'er them lay;
> How, in some desperate feud of after-time
> He sheltered there a daughter of the clime,
> A foe beloved, and offspring of a foe,
> Saved by his tribe but for a captive's woe;
> How, when the storm of war was stilled, he led
> His island clan to where the waters spread
> Their deep-green shadow o'er the rocky door,
> Then dived—it seemed as if to rise no more:
> His wondering mates, amazed within their bark,
> Or deemed him mad, or prey to the blue shark;
> Rowed, round in sorrow the sea-girded rock,
> Then paused upon their paddles from the shock;
> When, fresh and springing from the deep, they saw
> A Goddess rise—so deemed they in their awe.
>                         (IV.9.195-212)

These anecdotes show that Neuha and Torquil occupy only a psychologically timeless present. There is a real time continuum, but Neuha deals with it mentally, in two ways. First, as we see above, she attenuates the terrors past and to come by couching them in romantic ballads. Second, as Byron reports with apparent misgiving, she simply forgets: 'She feared no ill, because she knew it not, / Or what she knew was soon—too soon—forgot' (II.7.149-50). She deliberately avoids paying attention to 'Experience, that chill touchstone, whose / Sad proof reduces all things from their hues' (II.7.147-48), and thus the narrator has a qualified view of the Islanders as 'more happy, if less wise' (II.11.269). Their culture has many favorable aspects when compared with the narrator's, but much of what is favorable is the product of ignorance, of a lack of critical awareness. Like Scott, Byron cannot endorse the concept of a successfully enclosed Romance culture. However exotic the Highlanders or Islanders may be, they are not unreal; but they are unrealistic in their outlooks.

The British naval vessel, the *Bounty,* whose course through South Sea waters opens the poem, represents a totally different life from that of Toobonai. The ship is not a complete world: it operates within an implied context of Admiralty directives, which are in turn the instrumentality for accomplishing broader objectives of the nation. But the ship gives in concentrated form an example of that large and complex organization of collective life, the modern European nation, and we see that this life is far removed from the carefree, undisciplined, and inconsequential life of Toobonai.

In the opening words of the poem, 'The morning watch was come; the vessel lay / Her course . . .,' we see that the world of the ship has a time frame, has men assigned to perform duties within that frame, and has a scheme of goal-directed movement. When we read that the ultimate authority on the ship, Captain Bligh, sleeps 'Secure in those by whom the watch was kept' (I.2.18), we see that the successful functioning of this world requires that each member fulfill the duty to which he has been assigned. To have fulfilled one's duty is to have earned a peaceful sleep like that of Bligh:

> His dreams were of Old England's welcome shore,
> Of toils rewarded, and of dangers o'er;
> His name was added to the glorious roll
> Of those who search the storm-surrounded Pole.
>                                   (I.2.19-22)

His native land is welcome to him, because he has served her, and she will reward him in gratitude. (As well, one can note, the objective of the voyage has been to serve civilization's quest for knowledge.)

There is a reverse process, of course, for those who shirk their duties: 'injured Navies urge their broken laws' (I.10.204), seek revenge by punishing those who have violated the laws constituting this world. It is a world which sanctions its own existence, then, by depriving those who have threatened it of theirs.

Byron's picture of European civilization as expressed in the life of the *Bounty* should remind us of Francis Foscari's necessary compromises with his humanity in order to serve the state. Self-denial is the price exacted to maintain civilization (as Freud postulated in *Civilization and Its Discontents*), and requires a suppression of deep human longings which, as Byron says, 'ages have not yet subdued / In man' (I.2.37-38). It is too high a price for those members of the crew led by Christian in mutiny.

Instead of a life of self-denying toil under law, the mutineers want 'no master save . . . mood' (I.2.38), rewards without the necessity of payment (I.6), and 'happy shores without a law' (I.10.209): in short, they want to enter Europe's reverse-image world, Toobonai. But passing through the looking-glass is not so easily done, for it involves renouncing one's past, one's identity as constituted by the conditions of the life to which one was born. Byron argues that the initial circumstances of our lives go to condition our basic sense of right and wrong. But desiring that world is a weakness, a result of all the conditioning forces of life:

> Alas, such is our nature! all but aim
> At the same end by pathways not the same;
> Our means—our birth—our nation, and our name,
> Our fortune—Temper—even our outward frame,
> Are far more potent o'er our yielding clay
> Than aught we know beyond our little day.
> (I.6.115-20)

And this weakness is disciplined by an absolute, our sense of right and wrong:

> Yet still there whispers the small voice within,
> Heard through Gain's silence, and o'er Glory's din:
> Whatever creed be taught, or land be trod,
> Man's conscience is the Oracle of God.
> (I.6.121-24)

Neither rationalization nor geographical escape will allow escape from conscience (as Christian so fearfully shows).

The conflict on the *Bounty* is thus between behavior in accordance with objective forms (of law, reason) and behavior which obeys the deepest longings of the self. Byron's ambivalence about this split is revealed in his phrasing of an excuse for the mutineers to drink brandy in the heat of rebellion, 'Lest passion should return to reason's shoal' (I.6.100): passion is of the depths and reason of the shallows; depths suggest spiritual profundity but also unsafeness; the shallowness of the shoal suggests superficiality and an impediment to free movement but also the security of a known foundation. Each faction in the mutiny raises similar problems of evaluation.

Bligh as representative of order is not discussed in detail, except to be called 'The gallant Chief' (I.2.17), who has worked hard and sternly reproaches Christian for his breach of duty. But Byron treats Bligh and his 'faithful few' (I.7.125) favorably, with no negative shading. When thrust into an open boat, they are given 'that trembling vassal of the Pole— / The feeling compass—Navigation's soul' (I.5.95-96): the loyal crew are also trembling vassals before the Pole of authority, but in firm possession of their souls. In the arduous boat voyage, the virtues of Juan in a similar experience come into play again in 'Their manly courage even when deemed in vain' (I.9.180). And when they are returned to England, 'Roused Discipline aloud proclaims [the] cause' (I.10.203) of these tried and true men.

Where Bligh and his crew are submissive but right, Christian and his mutineers are freer but wrong. The action of mutiny is described in terms of excess: it is 'the drunken hour, / The Saturnalia of unhoped-for power' (I.5.83-84) which converts a 'proud vessel' into 'a moral wreck' (I.7.128). Such freedom outside the law is anarchy and in the face of Bligh's firmness it must assert itself through extremist measures:

> That savage spirit, which would lull by wrath
> Its desperate escape from Duty's path,
> Glares round thee, in the scarce believing eyes
> Of those who fear the- Chief they sacrifice:
> For ne'er can Man his conscience all assuage,
> Unless he drain the wine of Passion—Rage.
>                                      (I.3.59-64)

Rage, hate, passion, stern hearts, obduracy are Byron's terms for this extremism, and it is focussed in Christian.

His aim is 'to be, / In life or death, the fearless and the free' (III.6.163-64), but he knows how desperate a gamble lawlessness is for achieving that end. To Bligh's reproach at the moment of mutiny, Christian can answer only with an admission of guilt: 'Tis that! 'tis that! I am in hell! in hell!' (I.8.164). Christian is a true Byronic Hero, 'a figure of a higher order' (III.6.139) than the other mutineers, whose Promethean attempt to bring man the fire of Freedom has plunged him into perdition. That evil of willfulness we have seen in all Byronic Heroes is now depicted by Byron as in entropy, dying slowly. When the moment of punishment comes, Christian is moving gradually to a state of inanimacy,

> Like an extinct volcano in his mood;
> Silent, and sad, and savage,—with the trace
> Of passion reeking from his clouded face.
> (III.6.140-42)

He faces death 'Obdurate as a portion of the rock / Whereon he stood' (IV.11.278-79). In death, Christian is resolved back into the elements, 'With scarce a shred to tell of human form. . . . / The rest was nothing — save a life misspent, / And soul—but who shall answer where it went?' (IV.12.343, 351-52). Byron seems finally to have renounced the passionate Byronic Hero. The crew of the punitive expedition which comes after Christian 'firm . . . / To act whatever Duty bade them do,' sees him as 'This poor victim of self-will' (IV.12.281-82, 287). It is the epitaph for the Byronic Hero.

Christian was, however, 'aloof a little from the rest' (III.4.85), and did not express the whole human reality of the mutineers, for Byron is certainly ambivalent about them. Their depiction reveals a varied range of behavior and character types. One sailor shows 'repentant sympathy' (I.8.146) as Bligh is put into the boat. Two others, Ben Bunting and Jack Skyscrape (III. 18-21), are colorful comic characters, reminding one perhaps of Scott's comic minor figures (Evan Maccombich, Edie Ochiltree, Caleb Balderstone, Goose Gibby). And of course there is 'The fair-hair'd Torquil' (discussed below). On the whole, these 'rudest sea-boys' (I.6.lll) are heedless in their fight for lawless freedom. The rage of mutiny once over, they enjoy the pacific and humane values of Toobonai. When the punitive force comes, Torquil asserts: 'we'll make no running fight, for that were base,' to which Bunting replies, 'for that 'tis all the same to Ben' (II.21. 517, 519)—that is, Torquil will defend this new way of life nobly, but the typical sailor is less discriminating about the meaning of his actions. The mutineers as a group lack the discriminating moral conscience of a Christian: they are not leaders but the led. They wish merely to be exempted from their old culture, naively entertaining

> . . . the lingering hope, which deemed their lot Not pardoned, but unsought for or forgot,
> Or trusted that, if sought, their distant caves Might still be missed amidst the world of waves . . . .

(III.2.33-36)

They are, in short, ordinary men attempting to escape the fatality of modern civilization. Pathetic figures, their predicament reminds us of that described by one critic as an essential one of the Waverley novels: 'the valuable diversities and complexities of mankind asserting themselves against laws too abstract, too rigid, too impersonal.'[8]   British naval law does reach out to destroy or capture all the mutineers save Torquil.

We must conclude, I feel, that Byron sees the mutineers as admirable but pathetic, as responding to a human need (which is articulated by Christian) but unwise in their methods and unrealistic in their expectations.   In depicting Christian, Torquil, and Neuha as they grandly take a stand against their pursuers, Byron shows how wrong he now feels that mere act of rebellion, serving the self alone, to be:

> They stood, the three, as the three hundred stood
> Who dyed Thermopylae with holy blood.
> But, ah! how differentl 'tis the *cause* makes all,
> Degrades or hallows courage in its fall.
> O'er them no fame, eternal and intense,
> Blazed through the clouds of Death and beckon'd hence;
> No grateful country, smiling through her tears,
> Begun the praises of a thousand years;
> No nation's eyes would on their tomb be bent,
> No heroes envy them their monument;
> However boldly their warm blood was spilt,
> Their Life was shame, their Epitaph was guilt.
> And this they knew and felt, at least the one,
> The leader of the band he had undone.
>                              (IV.11.259-72)

Byron has now shown Toobonai clashing directly with Britain—that would be 'a sacrifice which were in vain; / For what were simple bow and savage spear / Against the arms which must be wielded here?' (IV.10.250-52). But he has denied that members of the modern world can move into the earlier world of Toobonai, not only because of the efficiency of British law enforcement, but because of the realities of the moral life. Oppression cannot be simply evaded but must be faced in wars of national liberation. Only here can victory be significant, because of value for all.

The different treatment accorded Torquil and Neuha—they do not feel their lives to be shameful—is the exception proving the rule. They are Byron's projection in the romance mode of a dreamed-of deliverance from the oppressive forces of modern history.

## (2) Romance and Reality

In Toobonai, Byron like Scott creates a culture which is only like a Romance world exotic in its contrast with modern civilization. The Romance of *The Island* lies in Torquil's successful entrance into Toobonai life (and conversely, in his successful escape from European life). To emphasize what he has done, Byron has, in the mutineers Christian and Torquil, brought together for the first time, as in a Scott novel, a Byronic Hero and a Waverley type of Hero. The Byronic Hero is destroyed both spiritually and physically in his attempt to escape the unsatisfactory aspects of his historical dilemma while Torquil is successful.

Torquil, compared to Christian, is a Juanesque hero. His portrait is complex only in its initial sketch, which is worth quoting in full:

8

And who is he? the blue-eyed northern child
Of isles more known to man, but scarce less wild;
The fair-hair'd offspring of the Hebrides,
Where roars the Fentland with its whirling seas;
Rocked in his cradle by the roaring wind,
The tempest-born in body and in mind,
His young eyes opening on the ocean-foam
Had from that moment deem'd the deep his home,
The giant comrade of his pensive moods,
The sharer of his craggy solitudes,
The only Mentor of his youth where'er
His bark was borne; the sport of wave and air;
A careless thing, who placed his choice in chance,
Nursed by the legends of his land's romance;
Eager to hope, but not less firm to bear,
Acquainted with all feelings save despair.
Placed in the Arab's clime, he would have been
As bold a rover as the sands have seen,
And braved their thirst with as enduring lip
As Ishmael, wafted on his Desert-Ship;
Fix'd upon Chili's shore, a proud cacique;
On Hellas' mountains, a rebellious Greek;
Born in a tent, perhaps a Tamerlane;
Bred to a throne, perhaps unfit to reign.
For the same soul that rends its path to sway,
If reared to such, can find no further prey
Beyond itself, and must retrace its way,
Plunging for pleasure into pain: the same
Spirit which made a Nero, Rome's worst shame,
A humbler state and discipline of heart

Had form'd his glorious namesake's counterpart;
But grant his vices, grant them all his own,
How small their theatre without a throne!

9

Thou smilest; — these comparisons seem high
To those who scan all things with dazzled eye;
Linked with the unknown name of one whose doom
Has nought to do with glory or with Rome,
With Chili, Hellas, or with Araby;—
Thou smilest?—Smile; 'tis better thus than sigh;
Yet such he might have been; he was a man,
A soaring spirit, ever in the van,
A patriot hero or despotic chief,
To form a nation's glory or its grief,
Born under auspices which make us more
Or less than we delight to ponder o'er.
But these are visions; say, what was he here?
A blooming boy, a truant mutineer:
The fair-hair'd Torquil, free as ocean's spray,
The husband of the bride of Toobonai.

(Canto II)

Close inspection of these stanzas reveals a roster of Byron's heroes:
Childe Harold/Narrator (11.168-76), Juan (11.177-78), the Oriental tale
heroes, and Sardanapalus (11.179-90). Torquil enjoys only the favorable
characteristics and circumstances which can be imagined for these heroes:
a review of what is favorable will show the Romance life Byron has
created for Torquil.

Like the narrator of *Childe Harold*, Torquil finds 'the deep'—the
sublime aspects of nature in mountain and ocean—his home. His love for
Neuha is sublime, too, in its transcendence of natural mutability. When
the sun sets, the two lovers are surprised and look 'for light into each
other's eyes' (III.15.367), for that light outlasts the sun's merely natural
capacity. Whereas Juan's apparently ideal love relation with Haide'e was
subject to both internal and external dynamics of corruption and decay,
Torquil's love is literally a world apart. It is Dryden's *All for Love* made
impossibly present, and the connection with *Sardanapalus* is pointed when
Byron writes of Torquil that

His heart was tamed to that voluptuous state,
At once Elysian and effeminate,
Which leaves no laurels o'er the Hero's urn. . . . .

(II.13.312-14)

This last statement expresses clearly Byron's ambiguous valuation of Torquil: he has attained a supramundane (Elysian) love, but has thereby forfeited a mundane identity. That is, Torquil has simply been removed from the context of process, natural and historical, wherein experience and identity are earned. Despite his being 'a soaring spirit,' he will not develop for better or worse, to be 'A patriot hero or despotic chief.'

Byron finally removes his gentle Torquil from a deathly combat to which he is not suited, and by his dive into the sea with Neuha, where he becomes 'the Pilgrim of the Deep' (IV.5.95), Torquil is reborn into a new life. This survival is similar in some respects to that achieved by Henry Morton. In *Old Mortality*, the dominance of 'mortality,' of that fatedness to death which Morton's involvement with Burley represents, is broken symbolically by Morton's leap from a cliff away from the mad and menacing Burley. One critic observes that

> The leap is literally and symbolically his leap back to life. It is his final refusal to fight, his own daring evasion of evil, his refusal to betray or take action against his father's preserver.[9]

In another respect, Byron's resolution is the opposite of Scott's. The Waverley Hero achieves a Romance survival within history, whereas Torquil achieves a Romance survival by going outside it. What is significant about *The Island*, though, is that Byron should project any kind of survival at all. The work was a daydream, amidst other involvements, of the best that he had found in life. It is in *The Island* that Byron makes the long personal apostrophe.to 'the Highlands' swelling blue' (II.12.280; quoted in full in Chapter ONE above), and asserts that 'nature's native scenes [are] / Loved to the last whatever intervenes / Between us and our childhood's sympathy.' So much had 'intervened' for Byron that the realm of freedom existed mainly in a memory of his own youth and in the fantasy of the youthful world of Toobonai. But it could exist again, if history were to come full cycle.

That Byron could create a knowingly positive fiction of survival was an earnest of that hopefulness which kept him and his Juan moving forward. He could not depict a survival within history when that could be proved only in the living. Like a young Waverley Hero, Byron in going to Greece was accepting an involvement in history which might prove to have other than a tragic ending.

## Afterword

Torquil's escape was not Byron's. On the contrary, his way was back into the turmoil of modern Europe. But *The Island* did allow Byron to affirm valuable allegiances: to his own Scottish boyhood with its refreshing love of the dark glories of the rugged Highlands; to the cause of national freedom as the closest realization of human freedom; and to the self-denying commitment required to effect true changes in the history of an oppressed mankind.

While chafing at the injustices in the Britain of his day, Byron seemed fully reconciled to the Union of 1707.[10] Hence he eulogized earlier fighters for freedom, the most pertinent of which, to his boyhood sympathies, were the Scots who had, moreover, fought an oppressive England. In the midst of his exile, Scott's novels helped Byron maintain a link with his own youth, a time of high hopes and Romantic ideals.

*In The Island*, Byron celebrated fighting for one's country as did those "Who dyed Thermopylae with holy blood" (IV.11.260). National independence he saw as the most valid sanction for heroic endeavor, and he found scope for this at first and to a lesser degree, in Italy, but finally— and in the eyes of the world, gloriously— in Greece.

The heroism adumbrated in *Don Juan*, stoical endurance in the service of humanity, was exemplified by Byron in Greece. The Byron there was not the flamboyant egocentrist he is often popularly supposed but, more in the fashion of an Edward Waverley or a Henry Morton, a cool discipliner of his troops. Byron had found freedom, not in the absolute, metaphysical sense, but in the engaged, mundane, and historically significant sense toward which we have seen his works developing:

> The sword, the banner, and the field,
> Glory and Greece, around me see!
> The Spartan, borne upon his shield,
> Was not more free.
> ('On This Day I Complete My Thirty-Sixth Year')

When Byron died in the midst of the Greek campaign, Scott could appreciate how consistently his whole life had tended to this consummation: 'His foot was always in the arena, his shield hung always in the lists. . . .'[11]  Scott himself had had no small part in Byron's full entrance into battle.

# Notes

[1] Robert F. Gleckner, *Byron and the Ruins of Paradise* (Baltimore: Johns Hopkins Press, 1967), p. 347.

[2] Q.v. Clifford Michael Byrne, 'Lord Byron: His Classical Republicanism, Cyclical View of History, and Their Influence on His Work,' *DA*. XXIV (1963), 282.

[3] *A Critical History of English Literature*, 2 vols. (New York: Ronald Press, 1960), II, 835-36. However, Scott had a critically qualified view of 'the traditional kind of heroism,' as noted in Ch. FOUR above.

[4] Francis Hart, *Scott's Novels; The Plotting of Historic Survival* (Charlottesville: Univ. Press of Virginia, 1966), p. 317.

[5] *Scott*, I, 670.

[6] *BLJ*. 10, 90 (to Leigh Hunt, 25 Jan. 1823).

[7] *Politics in English Romantic Poetry* (Cambridge, Mass.: Harvard Univ. Press, 1970), p. 225.

[8] Kroeber, *Romantic Narrative Art*, p. 186.

[9] Hart, *Scott's Novels*, p. 84.

[10] See ftnt 53, Ch. ONE.

[11] Robert Cadell, 'The Death of Lord Byron,' *The Miscellaneous Prose Works*, 6 vols. (Edinburgh: Cadell, 1834), IV, 347.

# APPENDIX A

# BYRON'S REFERENCES TO SCOTT NOVELS AND MISCELLANEA

(in the letters and miscellaneous prose, *BLJ*, all to Murray unless noted otherwise; parenthetical dates are year of publication of a Scott novel)

24 July 1814—*Waverley* (1814) has been read (hereafter, 'read')

2 Feb 1815—eager to receive *Guy Mannering* (1815)

30 Sep 1816—in Diodati, plans to take *The Antiquary* (1816) to Mme.de Stael

5 Oct 1816—*Antiquary* not as good as *Waverley* or *Guy Mannering* 'but much above all the last twenty years—'

24 Dec 1816—quotes from *Waverley* (to Thomas Moore)

19?Feb 1817—tells Augusta Leigh 'I am not "P.P."', the pseudonymous author (Peter Pattieson) of *The Black Dwarf* (1816)

3 Mar 1817—*Quarterly* review *of Childe Harold* III read 9 May 1817, *The Black Dwarf* and *Old Mortality* (both 1816, as First Series of 'Tales of My Landlord') read

9 May 1817—'the "Tales of My Landlord" I have read with great pleasure.'; and sees why his sister and aunt think he wrote them

4 June 1817—in Rome, finally has received forwarded copies of 'Tales of My Landlord'

17 July 1818—*Rob Roy* (1817) read

1 Mar 1820—refers to *The Bride of Lammermoor* and *A Legend of Montrose*, asks about *Ivanhoe* (all 1819)

15 Mar 1820—has read 'Bridal of Triermain' and 'Harold the Dauntless' (poems)

29 Mar 1820—quotes from *Lammermoor*

14 Apr 1820—refers to a character in *Montrose*, also on 16 Apr, 24 Apr (to Douglas Kinnaird)

16 Apr 1820—quotes from *Old Mortality*

23 Apr 1820—quotes from *Rob Roy* and *Waverley*, refers to *Ivanhoe* and *The Monastery* (1820)

8 May 1820—'Send me Scott's novels'

7 June 1820—receives *Ivanhoe*

8 Aug 1820—refers to a character in *Montrose*

12 Aug 1820—wants *Monastery*, 20 Aug repeats request

16 Aug 1820—receives *The Abbot* (1820), quotes 20 Aug, quotes 25 Aug (to Augusta Leigh)

20 Aug 1820—has *Abbot* (to Richard Belgrave Hoppner)

4 Sept 1820—receives *Monastery*, 'that Grand Desideratum of the last Six Months', quotes 9 Sept

7 Sep 1820—quotes from *Waverley* ('I have read all Scott's novels at least fifty times')

5 Jan 1821—Conclusion of 'Third Series of Tales' reread (probably *Ivanhoe*), ('I have read all the others forty times')

7 Jan 1821—refers to *Kenilworth* (1821)

8 Jan 1821—*Rob Roy* reread

24 Jan 1821—quotes from *Black Dwarf*

2 Feb 1821—quotes from *Waverley*

7 Feb 1821—quotes from *Old Mortality* and *Rob Roy*

1 Mar 1821—requests *Waverley*, *Antiquary*, and *Mannering* for rereading

25 Mar 1821—quotes from *Montrose* and *Waverley*

26 Apr 1821—praises *Kenilworth*

1 May 1821—refers to *Lammermoor*

6 Oct 1821—quotes from *Waverley*

15 Oct 1821—quotes from *Antiquary* (twice)

12 Nov 1821—refers to *Monastery* and *Abbot*

12 Jan 1822—quotes from *The Heart of Midlothian* (1818) (twice) and *Rob Roy*, awaits *The Pirate* (1821)

5 Feb 1822—refers to character in *Kenilworth*

4 May 1822—quotes from *Waverley* and *Rob Roy*

23 Sept 1822—receives Scott's gift of *Halidon Hill* (a drama)

7 Mar 1823—requests *Peveril of the Peak* 1823); allegedly quotes from it in this year (to Lady Blessington)

17 Mar 1823—awaits *Perveril* (to John Hunt)

7 Apr 1823—quotes from *Antiquary*

19 Apr 1823—quotes from *Midlothian* (to John Hunt)

21 May 1823—quotes from *Montrose* (to John Bowring)

12 Aug 1823—quotes from *Midlothian* and *Quentin Durward* (1823)

19 Mar 1823—probable reference to *Antiquary*

24 Oct 1823—quotes from *Waverley*

28 Dec 1823—Hancock reports that the day before leaving Argostoli, Byron was reading *Quentin Durward*

4 Mar 1824—possible reference to *Quentin Durward*

**Note**:  The only Scott novels published in Byron's lifetime that he seemed unaware of were *The Fortunes of Nigel* (1822), *St. Ronan's Well* (1823), and *Redgauntlet* (1824).  Byron died in April 1824.

# APPENDIX B

# SCOTT'S DOGGEREL PRECURSOR
# TO DON JUAN

'For amusement and to help a little publication that is going on here I have spun a doggrel[sic] tale called *The Search after Happiness,*' Scott wrote to J. B. S. Morritt in January 1817.[1]  The work appeared in John Ballantyne's weekly pamphlet, *The Sale-Room,* No. 5, 1 February 1817 and, as Edgar Johnson observes, 'anticipates some of the mocking gaiety if not the glitter Byron would later bring to his *Don Juan.*'[2]

Scott uses verse stanzas of irregular length, with couplet-rhymed lines, and so does not formally anticipate Byron's *ottava rima* satires (which begin with Beppo, written in the autumn of 1818). But in manner the work draws from the same Italian comic epic tradition which, both in itself and by way of John Hookham Frere's *Whistlecraft,* had led directly to Byron's *ottava rima* style.[3] Casti is a direct influence, for his *La Camiscia Magica* provided Scott's story line. We know that Byron enjoyed Casti's works, and that the reading of *Whistlecraft* in September 1817 spurred him immediately to the writing of *Beppo.*[4]  Whether he had seen or ever saw *Search,* published over seven months earlier, is not known, but we do know he had met Scott in April 1815 and immensely enjoyed his company and writing.  Here it may be the case, as Jorge Borges has so shrewdly observed, that 'every writer creates his own precursors.'[5]  *Search* is of note chiefly in demonstrating that Byron and Scott could share a similar sense of humor, technique, and overall narrative structure, as the following remarks, made with Byron's style in mind, may indicate.

*Search* is the story of a Sultan, ill from melancholy, who is told he can be cured by finding and wearing the shirt of a happy man.  As in *Don Juan,* the protagonist then travels through various countries of the Mediterranean and Europe, ending in Great Britain. National characteristics are emphasized in several of the countries and reference to historical events (Waterloo) is made. Scott's narrator jests at his readers' and nation's tastes (and uses *a* bit of outrageous rhyme in the process):

Yet fear not, ladies, the *naive* detail
Given by the natives of that land canorous; Italian license loves to leap the
pale,
We Britons have the fear of shame before us,
And, if not wise in mirth, at least must be decorous.
(11. 5-9)

He is cheerfully digressive, at the same time drawing attention to his own
art:

This Solimaun Serendib had in sway—
And where's Serandib? may some critic say.—
Good lack, mine honest friend, consult the chart,
Scare not my Pegasus before I start! If Rennell has it not, you'll find
mayhap
The isle laid down in Captain Sindbad's map— Famed mariner, whose
merciless narrations
Drove every friend and kinsman out of patience,
Till, fain to find a guest who thought them shorter,
He deigned to tell them over to a porter—
The last edition see, by Long, and Co.,
Rees, Hurst, and Orme, our fathers in the Row.
(11. 28-39)

Concepts of the physical and spiritual are juxtaposed with amusing
incongruity (think of Byron's sermons and soda water):

A sort of stimulant which has its uses
To raise the spirits and reform the juices;
(11. 42-43)

and of anticlimax:

These counsels sage availed not a whit,
And so the patient—as is not uncommon
Where grave physicians lose their time and wit—
Resolved to take advice of an old woman. . . .
(11. 126-29)

The ending of *Search* provides a humorous letdown—similar to the
revelation at the end of *Don Juan* Canto XVI that the 'ghost,' unhooded, is
her Grace, Fitz-Fulke; and depends on the historical conditioning of the
people involved. A happy man is finally found, in Ireland. But John Bull
had 'For a long space . . . with words of thunder, / Hard looks, and harder
knocks, kept Paddy under' (11. 317-19):

They seized, and they floored, and they
stripped him—Alack!
Up—bubboo! Paddy had not—a shirt to his back!
(11. 345-46)

The tale as a whole, sharing Byron's satirical sense, gives us one more ground for that intimacy and delight he and Scott found in each other's company.

# Notes

[1] *The Letters of Sir Walter Scott*. Ed. J.G. Tait and W.M. Parker. 3 vols., Edinburgh: Oliver Boyd, 1939-47. IV, 383 (31 Jan 1817).

[2] Johnson, Edgar. *Sir Walter Scott: The Great Unknown*. 2 vols. New York: Macmillan, 1970. I, 563-64, and notes, lviii.

[3] Boyd, Elizabeth French. *Byron's Don Juan: A Critical Study*. 1945. Rpt. New York: Humanities Press, 1958. pp. 10, 12, and *passim*.

[4] Boyd, p. 10

[5] Borges, Jorge. 'Kafka and His Precursors,' in *Labyrinths* (New York: New Directions, 1962), p. 201.

# BIBLIOGRAPHY

## Primary

**(a) Byron**

Coleridge, Ernest Hartley, ed. *The Works of Lord Byron: Poetry*. 6 vols. London: John Murray, 1898-1904.

Lovell, Ernest J., Jr., ed. *His Very Self and Voice: Collected Conversations of LordByron*. New York: Macmillan, 1954.

—. *Medwin's Conversations of Lord Byron*. Princeton: Princeton Univ. Press, 1966.

—. *Lady Blessington's Conversations of Lord Byron*. Princeton: Princeton Univ. Press, 1969.

Murray, John, ed. *Lord Byron's Correspondence*. 2 vols. London: John Murray, 1922.

Nicholson, Andrew, ed. *Lord Byron: The Complete Miscellaneous Prose*. Oxford: Oxford Univ. Press, 1991.

—. *The Letters of John Murray to Lord Byron*. Liverpool: Liverpool Univ. Press, 2007.

McGann, Jerome J., ed. *Lord Byron: The Complete Poetical Works*. Oxford: Oxford U.P., 1980-93.

Marchand, Leslie A., ed. *Byron's Letters and Journals*. 16 vols. Cambridge: Harvard Univ. Press, 1973-1982.

Prothero, Rowland E., ed. *The Works of Lord Byron: Letters and Journals*. 7 vols. London: John Murray, 1898-1901.


**(b) Scott**

Cadell, Robert. *The Miscellaneous Prose Works of Sir Walter Scott*. 6 vols. Edinburgh: Cadell, 1834.

Grierson, H. H. C. et al. *The Letters of Sir Walter Scott*. 12 vols. London: Constable, 1932-37.

Laing, D., ed. *Waverley Novels*. Centenary Edition. 25 vols. Edinburgh: Black, 1870-71.

Scudder, *Horace E., ed. The Complete Poetical Works of Sir Walter Scott*. Boston: Houghton Mifflin, 1900.

Tait, J. G. and W. M. Parker. *The Journal of Sir Walter Scott*. 3 vols. Edinburgh: Oliver & Boyd, 1939-47.

Williams, Ioan, ed. *Sir Walter Scott on Novelists and Fiction*. London: Routledge, 1968.

## Secondary

Alter, Robert. *Rogue's Progress*. Cambridge, Mass.: Harvard Univ. Press, 1964.

Ball, Margaret. *Sir Walter Scott as a Critic of Literature*. 1907; rpt. Port Washington, N.H.: Kennikat Press, 1966.

Ball, Patricia M. *The Central Self: A Study in Romantic and Victorian Imagination*. London: Athlone Press, 1968.

Barton, Anne. 'Byron and the Mythology of Fact.' *Nottingham Byron Lecture*. Nottingham, England: Univ. of Nottingham, 1968.

Bayley, John. *The Romantic Survival: A Study in Poetic Evolution*. London: Constable, 1957.

Beebe, Maurice. *Ivory Towers and Sacred Founts: The Artist as Hero in Fiction from Goethe to Joyce*. New York: New York Univ. Press, 1964.

Bloom, Harold. *The Visionary Company: A Reading of English Romantic Poetry*. 2nd ed. Ithaca, N.Y.: Cornell Univ. Press, 1971.

Bostetter, Edward E. *Introduction to George Gordon, Lord Byron; Selected Works*. 2nd ed. New York: Holt, 1972.

—. *The Romantic Ventriloquists: Wordsworth, Coleridge, Keats, Shelley, Byron*. Seattle: Univ. of Washington Press, 1963.

Bottrall, Ronald. 'Byron and the Colloquial Tradition in English Poetry.' *The Criterion* 18 (1939), 204-24.

Bowra, C. M. *The Romantic Imagination*. London: Oxford Univ. Press, 1950.

Boyd, Elizabeth French. *Byron's Don Juan: A Critical Study*. 1945; rpt. New York: Humanities Press, 1958.

Buchan, John. *Sir Walter Scott*. London: Cassell, 1932.

Bushnell, Nelson S. 'Walter Scott's Advent as a Novelist of Manners.' *Studies in Scottish Literature*, 1 (July 1963), 15-34.

Butler, E. M. *Byron and Goethe: Analysis of a Passion*. London: Bowes, 1956.

Buxton, John. *Byron and Shelley: The History of a Friendship*. London: Macmillan, 1968.

Byrne, Clifford Michael. 'Lord Byron: His Classical Republicanism, Cyclical View of History, and Their Influence on His Work.' *DA*. 24 (1963), 282. Vanderbilt.

Calder, Angus and Jennie. *Scott*. London: Evans, 1969.

Calder, Angus, ed. *Byron and Scott: Radical or Dandy?* Eninburgh: Edinburgh U.P., 1989.

Carlyle, Thomas. 'Characteristics' (1831), *The Works of Thomas Carlyle.* Ed. H. D. Traill. Centenary Edition. New York: Scribner's, 1896-99. XXVIII, 1-43.

Carruthers, Gerard and Rawes, Alan, eds. *English Romanticism and the Celtic World.* Cambridge: Cambridge U.P., 2003.

Carter, Ernest John. 'Byron's Historical Imagination: The Poetry of Byron Seen in Relation to Pessimistic Attitudes in Eighteenth-Century History.' *DA*, 28 (1967). Claremont.

Chambers, R. W. 'Ruskin (and Others) on Byron.' *English Association Pamphlet no.* 62, November 1925.

Chew, Samuel. *The Dramas of Lord Byron.* Baltimore: Johns Hopkins Press, 1915.

Clubbe, John. 'Byron and Scott.' *Texas Studies in Language and Literature*, 2003.

Cockshut, A. O. J. *The Achievement of Walter Scott.* London: Collins, 1969.

Cooke, Michael G. *The Blind Kan Traces the Circle: On the Patterns and Philosophy of Byron's Poetry.* Princeton: Princeton Univ. Press, 1969.

Crawford, Thomas. *Scott.* Edinburgh: Oliver & Boyd, 1965.

Cusac, Marian H. *Narrative Structure in the Novels of Sir Walter Scott.* The Hague: Mouton, 1969.

Daiches, David. 'Scott's Achievement as a Novelist.' *Literary Essays.* Edinburgh: Oliver & Boyd, 1956.

—. *A Critical History of English Literature.* 2 vols. New York: Ronald Press, 1960.

Davie, Donald. *The Heyday of Sir Walter Scott.* London: Routledge, 1961.

—. 'The Poetry of Sir Walter Scott.' *Proceedings of the British Academy,* 47 (1961), 61-75.

Devlin, D. D. *The Author of Waverley: A Critical Study of Walter Scott.* London: Macmillan, 1971.

—. ed. *Walter Scott; Modern Judgments.* London: Macmillan, 1968.

Doherty, Francis M. *Byron.* London: Evans, 1968.

Dowden, Wilfred S. 'The Consistency in Byron's Social Doctrine.' *Rice Institute Pamphlet, 37, no. 3* (October 1950), 18-44.

du Bos, Charles. *Byron and the Need of Fatality.* 1932; trans. Ethel Colburn Mayne. New York: Haskell House, 1970.

Duckworth, Alistair M. *The Improvement of the Estate: A Study of Jane Austen's Novels.* Baltimore: Johns Hopkins Univ. Press, 1971.

Eliot, T. S. 'Byron.' *From Anne to Victoria: Essays by Various Hands*.
    Ed. Bonamy Dobree. London: Cassell, 1937.
—. 'Byron.' *On Poetry and Poets*. Rev. ed. London: Faber, 1957.
Elledge, W. Paul. *Byron and the Dynamics of Metaphor*. Nashville:
    Vanderbilt Univ. Press, 1968.
Erdman, David V. 'Byron and The New Force of the People.' *Keats-
    Shelley Journal* 11 (Winter 1962), 47-64.
Erikson, Erik H. *Identity: Youth and Crisis*. New York: W. W. Norton,
    1968.
—. *Young Man Luther: A Study in Psychoanalysis and History*. New
    York: W. W. Norton, 1958.
Fleishman, Avrom, *The English Historical Novel: Walter Scott to Virginia
    Woolf*. Baltimore: Johns Hopkins Press, 1971.
—. *A Reading of Mansfield Park*. Minneapolis: Univ. of Minnesota Press,
    1967.
Foakes, R. A. *The Romantic Assertion; A Study in the Language of
    Nineteenth-Century Poetry*. New Haven: Yale Univ. Press, 1958.
French, Richard. 'The Religion of Sir Walter Scott.' *Studies in Scottish
    Literature 2* (July 1964), 32-44.
Fuess, Claude M. *Lord Byron as a Satirist in Verse*. 1912; rpt. New York:
    Russell, 1959.
Garber, Frederick. 'Self, Society, Value, and the Romantic Hero.'
    *Comparative Literature 19*, no. 4 (Fall 1967), 321-33.
Gleckner, Robert F. *Byron and the Ruins of Paradise*. Baltimore: Johns
    Hopkins Press, 1967.
Goode, Clement Tyson. *Byron as Critic*. 1923; rpt. New York: Haskell
    House, 1964.
Gordon, Robert C. *Under Which King? A Study of the Scottish Waverley
    Novels*. Edinburgh: Oliver & Boyd, 1969.
Grierson, Sir Herbert J. C. *Sir Walter Scott, Bart.: A New Life,
    Supplementary to, and Corrective o f, Lockhart's Biography*. London:
    Constable, 1938.
Hart, Francis. *Scott's Novels: The Plotting of Historic Survival*.
    Charlottesville: Univ. Press of Virginia, 1966.
Hassler, Donald M. *'Marino Faliero, the Byronic Hero, and Don Juan.'
    Keats-Shelley Journal* 14 (Winter 1965), 55-64.
Hauser, Arnold. *The Social History of Art*. Trans. Stanley Goodman. 2
    vols. New York: Knopf, 1952.
Hazlitt, William. *The Spirit of the Age: Or Contemporary Portraits*.
    1825; rpt. London: Oxford Univ. Press, 1954.

Hillhouse, James T. *The Waverley Novels and Their Critics.* Minneapolis: Univ. of Minnesota Press, 1936.

Hirsch, E. D., Jr. 'Byron and the Terrestrial Paradise.' *From Sensibility to Romanticism: Essays Presented to Frederick _W. Pottle.* Ed. Frederick W. Hilles and Harold Bloom. New York: Oxford Univ. Press, 1965.

Horn, Andres. Byron's *Don Juan and the Eighteenth-Century English Novel.* Bern: A. Francke, 1962.

Hume, Robert D. 'The *Island* and the Evolution of Byron's Tales. *Romantic and Victorian; Studies in Memory of William H. Marshall.* Ed. W. Paul Elledge and Richard L. Hoffman. Rutherford, N.J.: Fairleigh Dickinson Univ. Press, 1971.

Jack, Ian. *English Literature: 1815-32.* Oxford: Oxford Univ. Press, 1963.

Johnson, E. D. H. 'Don Juan in England.' *ELH. 11* (1944), 135-53.

—. 'A Political Interpretation of Byron's *Marino Faliero.*' *Modern Language Quarterly, 3* (1942), 417-25.

Johnson, Edgar. 'Scott and Dickens: Realist and Romantic.' *Victorian Newsletter*, no. 27 (Spring 1965), pp. 9-11.

—. *Sir Walter Scott: The Great Unknown.* 2 vols. New York: Macmillan, 1970.

Joseph, M. K. *Byron the Poet.* London: Gollancz, 1964.

Keats, John. *The Letters of John Keats, 1814-1821.* Ed. H. E. Rollins. 2 vols. Cambridge, Mass.: Harvard Univ. Press, 1958.

Keith, Christina. *The Author of Waverley: A Study in the Personality of Sir Walter Scott.* London: Robert Hale, 1964.

Kernan, Alvin B. *The Plot of Satire.* New Haven: Yale Univ. Press, 1965.

Kirk, Russell. *The Conservative Mind.* London: Faber, 1954.

Knight, G. Wilson. *Lord Byron: Christian Virtues.* New York: Barnes & Noble, 1953.

Kroeber, Karl. *Romantic Narrative Art.* Madison: Univ. of Wisconsin Press, 1960.

Lauber, John. *Sir Walter Scott.* New York: Twayne, 1966.

Lockhart, John Gibson. *John Bull's Letter to Lord Byron.* Ed. Alan Lang Strout. 1821; rpt. Norman, Okla.: Univ. of Oklahoma Press, 1947.

—. *Memoirs of the Life of Sir Walter Scott, Bart.* Author's Edition, 1839; rpt. Edinburgh: Black, 1871.

Lovell, Ernest J., Jr. *Byron: The Record of a Quest: Studies in a Poet's Concept and Treatment of Nature.* Austin: Univ. of Texas Press, 1949.

Lukacs, Georg. *The Historical Novel.* 2nd ed. Trans. Hannah and Stanley Mitchell. London: Merlin Press, 1962.

MacCarthy, Fiona. *Byron: Life and Legend.* New York: Farrar, Strauss and Giroux, 2002.

McGann, Jerome J. *Fiery Dust: Byron's Poetic Development.* Chicago: Univ. of Chicago Press, 1968.

McLaren, Moray. *Sir Walter Scott: The Man and Patriot.* London: Heinemann, 1970.

Marchand, Leslie. *Byron; A Biography.* 3 vols. New York: Knopf, 1957.

—. Byron's *Poetry; A Critical Introduction.* 1965; rpt. Cambridge, Mass.: Harvard Univ. Press, 1968.

Marjarum, Edward Wayne. *Byron as Skeptic and Believer.* 1938; rpt. New York: Russell, 1962.

Marshall, William H. Introduction. *Selected Poems and Letters of Byron.* Boston: Houghton Mifflin, 1968.

—. *The Structure of Byron's Major Poems.* Philadelphia: Univ. of Pennsylvania Press, 1962.

Mayhead, Robin. *Walter Scott.* Cambridge: Cambridge Univ. Press, 1973.

Mayne, Ethel Colburn. *Byron.* 2 vols. New York: Scribner, 1912.

Moore, Thomas. *Life of Lord Byron: With His Letters and Journals.* 1830; rpt. London: John Murray, 1854.

Nichol, John. *Byron.* London: Macmillan, 1880.

Nicholson, Harold. *Byron: The Last Journey: April 1823—April 1824.* 2nd ed. London: Constable, 1948.

Pearson, Hesketh. *Walter Scott: His Life and Personality.* London: Methuen, 1954.

Praz, Mario. *The Hero in Eclipse in Victorian Fiction.* London: Oxford Univ. Press, 1956.

Raleigh, John Henry. 'What Scott Meant to the Victorians.' *Victorian Studies* 7, no. 4 (June 1964), 7-34.

Raymond, Dora Neill. *The Political Career of Lord Byron.* London: Allen & Unwin, n.d.

Renwick, W. L. *English Literature; 1789-1815.* Oxford: Oxford Univ. Press, 1963.

—. *Sir Walter Scott Lectures: 1940-48.* Edinburgh: Edinburgh Univ. Press, 1950.

Ridenour, George M. 'Byron in 1816: Four Poems from Diodati.' *From Sensibility to Romanticism: Essays Presented to Frederick W. Pottle.* Ed. Frederick W. Hilles and Harold Bloom. New York: Oxford Univ. Press, 1965.

—. 'The Mode of Byron's *Don Juan.*' *PMLA,* 80 (1965), 442-46.

—. The Style of *Don Juan.* New Haven: Yale Univ. Press, 1960.

Rodway, Allan. *The Romantic Conflict.* London: Chatto & Windus, 1963.

Ruskin, John. 'Of Modern Landscape,' *Modern Painters* (1856), III, Part IV, Ch. xvi, in *The Works of John Ruskin*, ed. E. T. Cook and Alexander Wedderburn. Library Edition. 39 vols. London: Allen, 1903-12.

Rutherford, Andrew. *Byron: A Critical Study.* London: Oliver & Boyd, 1961.

Speer, Roderick S. 'Byron and the Scottish Literary Tradition.' *Studies in Scottish Literature.* Columbia: Univ. of South Carolina Press, 1979.

Speirs, John. *Poetry Towards Novel.* London: Faber, 1971.

—. *The Scots Literary Tradition.* 2nd ed. London: Faber, 1962.

Spilka, Mark. *Dickens and Kafka; A Mutual Interpretation.* London: D. Dobson, 1963.

Stephen, Leslie. 'Some Words about Sir Walter Scott.' 1871; rpt . *Hours in a Library.* London: Smith, Elder, 1875.

Synon, J. D. *Byron in Perspective.* London: M. Seeker, 1924.

Thorslev, Peter. *The Byronic Hero: Types and Prototypes.* Minneapolis: Univ. of Minnesota Press, 1962.

Trueblood, Paul G. *Lord Byron.* New York: Twayne, 1969.

Weinstein, Leo. *Metamorphoses of Don Juan.* Stanford, Calif.: Stanford Univ. Press, 1959.

Welsh, Alexander. *The Hero of the Waverley Novels.* New Haven: Yale Univ. Press, 1963.

Wells, Nannie Katherine. *George Gordon, Lord Byron: Scottish Genius.* Montreux, Switzerland: Michael Slains, 1966.

West, Paul. *Byron and the Spoiler's Art.* London: Chatto & Windus, 1960.

Wilkie, Brian. *Romantic Poets and the Epic Tradition.* Madison: Univ. of Wisconsin Press, 1965.

Wittig, Kurt. *The Scottish Tradition in Literature.* Edinburgh: Oliver & Boyd, 1958.

Woodring, Carl. *Politics and English Romantic Poetry.* Cambridge, Mass.: Harvard Univ. Press, 1970.

# INDEX

(of proper names and titles in the text)